Courageous
simplicity

More books by (in)courage

Take Heart: 100 Devotions to Seeing God When Life's Not Okay

LOOK FOR OTHER TITLES IN THIS SERIES:

Courageous Simplicity:
Abide in the Simple Abundance of Jesus

Courageous Joy:
Delight in God through Every Season
(March 2021)

Courageous Influence:
Embrace the Way God Made You for Impact
(July 2021)

Courageous Kindness:
Live the Simple Difference Right Where You Are
(October 2021)

For more resources, visit incourage.me

AN
(in)courage
BIBLE STUDY

courageous simplicity

ABIDE IN THE SIMPLE ABUNDANCE OF JESUS

Written by Ginger Kolbaba
and the (in)courage Community

Revell
a division of Baker Publishing Group
Grand Rapids, Michigan

Published by Revell
a division of Baker Publishing Group
PO Box 6287, Grand Rapids, MI 49516-6287
www.revellbooks.com

Printed in the United States of America

Library of Congress Cataloging-in-Publication Data

Names: Kolbaba, Ginger, editor.

Title: Courageous simplicity : living in the simple abundance of Jesus / Ginger Kolbaba, general editor.

Description: Grand Rapids, Michigan : Revell, a division of Baker Publishing Group, 2021. | "An (in)courage Bible study."

Identifiers: LCCN 2020020161 | ISBN 9780800738082 (paperback)

Subjects: LCSH: Simplicity—Religious aspects—Christianity.—Textbooks.

Classification: LCC BV4647.S48 C69 2021 | DDC 248.4—dc23

LC record available at https://lccn.loc.gov/2020020161

Unless otherwise indicated, all Scripture quotations are from the Christian Standard Bible®, copyright © 2017 by Holman Bible Publishers. Used by permission. Christian Standard Bible® and CSB® are federally registered trademarks of Holman Bible Publishers.

Scripture quotations labeled CEV are from the Contemporary English Version © 1991, 1992, 1995 by American Bible Society. Used by permission.

Scripture quotations labeled ESV are from The Holy Bible, English Standard Version® (ESV®), copyright © 2001 by Crossway, a publishing ministry of Good News Publishers. Used by permission. All rights reserved. ESV Text Edition: 2016

Scripture quotations labeled GNT are from the Good News Translation in Today's English Version-Second Edition. Copyright © 1992 by American Bible Society. Used by permission.

Scripture quotations labeled MSG are from THE MESSAGE, copyright © 1993, 1994, 1995, 1996, 2000, 2001, 2002 by Eugene H. Peterson. Used by permission of NavPress. All rights reserved. Represented by Tyndale House Publishers, Inc.

Scripture quotations labeled NASB are from the New American Standard Bible® (NASB), copyright © 1960, 1962, 1963, 1968, 1971, 1972, 1973, 1975, 1977, 1995 by The Lockman Foundation. Used by permission. www.Lockman.org

Scripture quotations labeled NET are from the NET Bible®, copyright © 1996–2016 by Biblical Studies Press, L.L.C. http://netbible.com. Used by permission. All rights reserved.

Scripture quotations labeled NIV are from the Holy Bible, New International Version®. NIV®. Copyright © 1973, 1978, 1984, 2011 by Biblica, Inc.™ Used by permission of Zondervan. All rights reserved worldwide. www.zondervan.com. The "NIV" and "New International Version" are trademarks registered in the United States Patent and Trademark Office by Biblica, Inc.™

Scripture quotations labeled NKJV are from the New King James Version®. Copyright © 1982 by Thomas Nelson. Used by permission. All rights reserved.

Scripture quotations labeled NLT are from the Holy Bible, New Living Translation, copyright © 1996, 2004, 2007, 2013, 2015 by Tyndale House Foundation. Used by permission of Tyndale House Publishers, Inc., Carol Stream, Illinois 60188. All rights reserved.

Scripture quotations labeled NOG are from the Names of God Bible (without notes) © 2011 by Baker Publishing Group. Used by permission.

Scripture quotations labeled TPT are from The Passion Translation®. Copyright © 2017 by BroadStreet Publishing® Group, LLC. Used by permission. All rights reserved.

Italics added to Scripture quotations reflect the author's emphasis.

(in)courage is represented by Alive Literary Agency, www.aliveliterary.com.

21 22 23 24 25 26 27   7 6 5 4 3 2 1

contents

introduction

finding the freedom and peace you long for

I'm just so *tired*."

How often have you uttered those words? Perhaps you look at the cluttered state of your home or your overcrowded schedule and long for space to breathe. Maybe your mind spins thinking about the needs in front of you or the dreams inside you, and hard as you try, so many things are still left undone. There are meetings and events and complicated relationships, running nonstop, chasing after want-tos and have-tos and unyielding expectations of others (and self). Oh, the constant expectations that never relent. Who has a moment to rest?

No wonder we're all so tired.

Our lives are complicated, fast-paced spectacles of never-ending multitasking. Technology demands constant access to us, begging for instant replies to every bing-bong alert. The scrolling pull of social media promises greater inspiration and deeper connection—but mostly leaves us empty, dissatisfied, longing.

Mother Teresa said, "The more you have, the more you are occupied. The less you have, the more free you are." Her words ring true in a deep place in our hearts—yet we still wonder whether we can actually live with less. Not just fewer possessions but fewer responsibilities and distractions. Is it even possible? It's an honest question to ask as we begin this study on courageous simplicity.

When we hear the word *simplicity*, often the first thing we think about is decluttering our garages, basements, and kids' rooms. For some of us, the Amish come to mind, and we desire the simpler lifestyle that community represents. We want to be free of all the frazzle and frenzy that seem to crowd our homes, workplaces, and schedules.

Less chaos. More peace. Is living this kind of good and simple life really within reach?

While organizing our homes and schedules is certainly a praiseworthy goal that can bring relief to our external turmoil, that's not the whole of simplicity. Simplicity isn't cleared countertops or an empty calendar. It goes much deeper than decluttering. It goes to the heart of our faith. Biblical simplicity calls for a courageous step toward pursuing a pure and simple devotion to God—keeping Him and His plans for our lives first in our hearts. Simplicity, very simply, comes from within.

Proverbs 13:7 tells us that "a pretentious, showy life is an empty life; a plain and simple life is a full life" (MSG). This study is all about what that simple and full life actually looks like and how Jesus meets us in it.

Simplicity isn't for the weak of heart. In fact, it calls for us to be on guard against the enemy of our souls. Paul wrote, "I am afraid that, as the serpent deceived Eve by his craftiness, your minds will be led astray from the *simplicity* and *purity* of devotion to Christ" (2 Cor. 11:3 NASB). It takes courage to live with eyes open to God's presence and heart surrendered to His leading.

Embracing simplicity doesn't mean we will never experience difficulties or overwhelming challenges. It means we choose to live with growing trust that God is in control of it all. With Christ as our guide, we can say, "It is well with my soul."

As you train in the spiritual practice of simplicity over the next six weeks, you will discover the God who loves you lavishly and wants to show you how to live present to His perfect peace. You will uncover biblical principles to help you embrace that you are enough and have enough in Him.

How to Use This Study

Courageous Simplicity is a great study for personal or small group use. If you're doing it with a group, we recommend allowing at least forty-five minutes for discussion, or more for larger groups. (We think groups of four to ten people work great!) Enhance your community study experience with our *Courageous Simplicity Leader Guide*. Go to www.incourage.me/leaderguides to download your free small group resources.

As you work through each day's study, there's a lot to take in. Don't feel like you have to do it all in one sitting. If you come to these pages with a *have-to-complete-it-all* mentality, that defeats the purpose of simplicity! Do some and ponder it. Ask God to reveal His insight and truth to you. Then listen as He speaks to you through His Word.

Each week focuses on a different aspect of simplicity:

- **Week 1** delves into a plea for simplicity—uncovering our longing for the simple life.
- **Week 2** looks at what drives us—what our treasures, time, and search for significance tell us about the state of our inner lives.
- **Week 3** examines how to live in the sacred present, responding to what drives us.
- **Week 4** explores the idea of "enough"—discovering who we are in Christ.
- **Week 5** motivates us to live with open hands and hearts—finding freedom in letting go of the things that hold us captive.
- **Week 6** shows us what living in the peace that comes through simplicity looks like, as we revel in the things that truly matter.

Each week has a cadence that will help you get the most out of this study:

- **Day 1** looks at our call to courageously explore that week's topic.
- **Day 2** spotlights how Jesus or another key biblical figure lived it out and what we can learn from that person.

- **Day 3** tackles what the world says about that week's topic.
- **Day 4** shows us God's heart for you in that topic.
- **Day 5** closes the week with motivation for becoming a courageous woman.

We at (in)courage are excited to begin this *Courageous Simplicity* journey with you. You'll see that each day opens with a story from one of our writers sharing her experience of pursuing simplicity. Our hope and prayer is that these stories will help you feel less alone and more seen as you look for God in your own story.

This study is yours, and there is freedom in how you use it. There are reflection questions throughout the study. If you're energized by spending time diving into every question and unpacking every verse, we believe you'll be blessed by them. If they're too much for you, skip what you need to with total freedom. There's no guilt when you choose to meet with Jesus and study His Word, however that looks for you.

Are you ready? Join us as we let go of the fast-paced life so we can embrace a God-paced life—one that brings the freedom and peace you've been longing for.

a plea for simplicity

The LORD is my shepherd;
I have what I need.

Psalm 23:1

D o we *have* to go back?"

My voice came out more like a whine as we packed up our camping gear. The next morning my husband and I would return home after spending a week at Yellowstone National Park, where we hung out watching the buffalo roam and the deer and the antelope play. The only have-tos had been deciding what we wanted to eat, where we wanted to hike, and what board game we wanted to play in the evenings. We experienced stunning views of nature and communed with each other and with God in the stillness and slowness of each day. My blood pressure held steady at "just right," I slept well each night, and I awoke refreshed and excited about the nonscheduled, uncomplicated promise of what the new day held for us. It was so simple, so wonderful.

Now, as I cleaned up around the campsite, the pressures of our schedules and busy, chaotic lifestyle back home threatened to take over my calm and peaceful state of mind.

"What if we just ran away?" I said, only half joking. I felt the serenity of the past seven days quickly fading—and we hadn't even ended our vacation yet!

I wanted a simpler existence like the one I'd tasted on our vacation. I yearned for a life that felt as though I controlled it more than it controlled me. A quieter life in which I could more easily listen to the Holy Spirit's voice. A life that allowed some breathing room, some sacred rhythms of ebb and flow instead of just *go, go . . . more, more . . . do, do . . . have, have . . . be, be.*

Why couldn't all of my life feel like it had during that week? I didn't necessarily want to quit my job, pack up my family, and move to the middle of the wilderness! But being able to slow down, savor life and relationships, and feel more at peace would have been nice.

—GINGER KOLBABA

Have you ever felt that way—longing for a simpler, less complicated life? Describe that here.

_____

_____

_____

_____

We often struggle to feel at peace, don't we? We multitask, we give, we serve. If something needs doing, we're usually the ones to step in, step up, and handle it—even when we don't have the time or energy. And we do it all with hearts that long to make everyone's lives a little better. We know the things we do are good—completing our work on time, making sure our children are well-fed and chauffeured to the right places at the right times, helping our friends when they most need us during a move or a breakup—yet all of those things are anything but simple. And in the midst of it all, we are tired, worn-out, exhausted.

When we think of having a peaceful, simpler life, three words often come to mind:

If only . . .
Someday . . .

How often have we wished our lives were simpler? *If only* I could complete this work project. *If only* my spouse would help around the house. *If only* my kids weren't involved in every activity. *If only* everyone didn't expect so much of me. *If only* others understood . . .

We often respond by encouraging ourselves to believe that *someday* it will be different. *Next week life will slow down after I . . . Next month when the kids . . . Let me just get past this project or to summer break . . .*

But next week, next month, next summer never seems to bring that desired outcome, because life fills up with the next thing and the next and the next.

Think about the *if-onlys* and *somedays* in your life. Write one or two of them here.

Wouldn't it be nice to experience a simpler life now rather than waiting for someday? The Bible tells us that we can experience those simpler things that really make life rich—and we can have them now. Psalm 23:1–3 is our guide.

Read Psalm 23:1–3 in one or two translations. (You can easily find various translations at BibleGateway.com or by downloading a Bible app on your phone.) Write out one of those translations here.

Underline the words or phrases that describe what God, our Good Shepherd, wants to provide us. What is it about those words or phrases that causes your heart to hope for something different?

_____

_____

_____

_____

As much as we yearn for a simpler life—which is a good thing—cutting back on activities, diminishing responsibilities, and enjoying more free time aren't what will bring the peace and freedom of true simplicity. Simplicity isn't really about where we live or what we do—it's about Who we do life with. Simplicity is about a Person. Psalm 23 tells us that "*the Lord* is my shepherd . . . *he* lets . . . *he* leads . . . *he* renews." Ultimately, we find simplicity in Jesus and following *His* leading.

> Simplicity isn't really about where we live or what we do—it's about Who we do life with.

We cannot expect to experience the simple life by merely offering a nod of acknowledgment to Christ before moving on with our own agendas. We must focus on Him and courageously seek His wisdom as we remove unnecessary distractions and make difficult decisions about what to keep in our lives.

What is a distraction you regularly battle?

_____

_____

_____

_____

Pursuing true simplicity is about pursuing Jesus. As Donald Whitney explains in *Simplify Your Spiritual Life,*

> We prune activities from our lives, not only to get organized, but also that our devotion to Christ and service for His kingdom will be more fruitful. We simplify, not merely to save time, but to eliminate hindrances to the time we devote to knowing Christ. All the reasons we simplify should eventually lead us to Jesus Christ.[1]

Simplicity doesn't just appear when we say no to one activity but fail to give our lives and schedules a major overhaul. Simplicity doesn't come when we decide to clear out our home of all its "junk" and donate or sell the excess. Minimizing busyness and possessions is great! But deep and abiding simplicity comes only when we "lay aside every hindrance . . . that so easily ensnares us" and "run with endurance the race that lies before us, keeping our eyes on Jesus, the source and perfecter of our faith" (Heb. 12:1–2). And that race is not the chaotic, fast-paced one that the world runs. It is not the *go, go . . . more, more . . . do, do . . . have, have . . . be, be* we mentioned earlier. It is "simply" to follow Jesus by listening to His voice and getting to know Him better.

Look up Proverbs 3:5–8. While this is a well-known passage, how could it affect the way you courageously embrace a simpler life?

What might God be leading you to give up in order to more fully pursue Him?

In what ways would embracing simplicity require courage? Why?

Reflect on this prayer and make it your own today:

Father, sometimes I feel so overwhelmed and exhausted by all the demands on me. I know this isn't how You want me to live or who You want me to be. Help me to pursue You above all— and in that pursuit, may I find the peace and contentment I long for. Thank You, my Great Shepherd. Amen.

He often withdrew to deserted places and prayed.

Luke 5:16

E very summer, I gather with friends for a retreat in a beautiful location, sometimes in the mountains, sometimes on a sandy beach. While we are together we talk deeply. We laugh big. We eat well. We sleep. We go on walks, shop, read, stretch.

We rest.

I'm a work-from-home mom of three little kids. I am usually unshowered and probably wearing something I picked up off the bedroom floor. If I get four uninterrupted hours of sleep in a row, I'm doing pretty well. Is it my norm to escape to a sun-drenched beach for rest? Um, no. My norm is three minutes to myself in the bathroom. And even that usually gets interrupted by a knock and a little voice on the other side of the door asking what I'm doing and when I will be out.

But those summer retreats awaken me to my rest deficit, because I forget. I forget that God calls us to peace. He calls us away from hustle and into rest.

Throughout Scripture, Jesus is caught escaping to quiet. He models for us, for our busy-doing-all-the-things selves, how to embrace the simplicity of rest. Real rest. The kind that allows us to catch our breath, to laugh, to feel peace. Jesus's life was full to the brim. He had a job, friends, family . . . Yet He also cleared away anything that hindered

Him from seeking quiet time with God, because He knew that rest matters to God.

And often we make it too hard. Rest does not need a beach or a spa. Rest doesn't even need a hot cup of coffee or a nap. Jesus shows us how to rest, and it's much simpler than we make it.

I can find and accept the rest that God offers when I make time for it. Chase it intentionally. Seek it diligently. Create moments for rest amidst the to-dos.

I'm learning that my summer friend retreats are a gift, but I can live simply and find rest even when there's not a sandy beach in sight. Jesus was a pro at seeking and finding His Father's presence. We can be too, exactly where we are.

—ANNA RENDELL

Has the busyness of life or a season where alone time is scarce ever made you forget that resting with God is possible? What has (or hasn't) worked well for you when it comes to stealing time away with God?

_____

_____

_____

_____

God's Word tells us to "make it your ambition to lead a quiet life" (1 Thess. 4:11 NIV). But how often we get caught up in the hustle and bustle!

That's why there's something so relatable about our Great Shepherd. Life was hectic and demanding for Him too. Jesus understood the whirlwind and burdens of regular life. *And yet* He still experienced a life of simplicity. We may be tempted to think that Jesus didn't have it as bad or as busy as we have it. After all, He lived two thousand years ago—no social media or traffic-jammed commutes or office politics, right? His life surely must have been simpler back then.

But let's actually take a closer look at Christ's earthly life and let that guide and mentor us. Throughout the Gospels we can find His real-life examples that show how we *can* have the simple life He invites us to. We can discover how to experience an even stronger faith and purpose in our daily lives, even in the midst of busy child-rearing years, work deadlines, marriage struggles, parenting challenges, volunteering activities, pursuing passions, starting ministries, caring for aging parents, and everything else that finds its way into our schedules. We just need to follow His example.

Look up at least three of the following verses. What do they have in common?

Matthew 14:13	Mark 1:35	Luke 22:41
Matthew 14:23	Mark 6:31	John 6:15

Jesus's life was full to the brim. He had responsibilities, friends, family. He kept busy teaching and training twelve disciples. He healed people. He navigated crowds that numbered into the thousands— and He fed them. He taught in the synagogues. Everywhere He went, throngs of people crowded in, making demands, pleading for His attention and help, following Him, wanting something from Him (or plotting to attack and betray Him).

And He handled it all—never turning people away in their desperation but having compassion on them. Though He was Messiah, fully

God, He also was fully human. And He navigated all of those demands in His humanness, just as we must. How did He do that?

We find Jesus's prescription for the simple life in the Gospels: He withdrew and prayed. Over and over, He escaped to the quiet.

Mark 6:31 gives us a good sense of just how chaotic Jesus's life was. What was the result of His being in such high demand?

_____

Describe a time when you felt swallowed by life's busyness or burdens—or how you feel if that's where you find yourself today.

_____

_____

_____

Reread Mark 6:31. What did Jesus invite the disciples to do in response to their stresses and burdens?

_____

_____

_____

It's an invitation He offers you today as well.

We'd love to get away for a while—who wouldn't? But often we make things too difficult. We excuse it away, claiming that we _would_ embrace simplicity, but our busyness and responsibilities aren't optional. After all, people are relying on us! And Anna's right: the simplicity of rest, peace, and contentment does not require a beach or a spa. It doesn't even need a hot cup of coffee or a nap. Jesus shows us how to embrace what we really need, and though it takes courage to extricate ourselves, it can be much simpler than we make it.

Throughout the Gospels, Jesus models for us, for our busy-doing-all-the-things selves, how to embrace simplicity, peace, and an abundant life—the kind that allows us to catch our breath, to laugh, and to come out on the other side of it rejuvenated and ready to face the demands that come our way. He shows us that simplicity isn't about avoiding the craziness of life—it's about being connected to the Father. Simple rest centers our souls so we can continue to meet the needs of those around us without losing our peace.

What's interesting to note is that when Jesus withdrew, the crowds followed Him (Mark 6:32–34). His retreat was often short-lived.

> **Simple rest centers our souls so we can continue to meet the needs of those around us without losing our peace.**

Does that sound familiar? You get a moment of peace and the next thing you know your kid is tapping on your shoulder demanding a snack. You get away alone and your mother texts you for help emailing some photos she's taken on her phone. You slip off to enjoy a cup of coffee and your boss calls asking if you can work overtime. Jesus gets it. He was so pressed in at times that He didn't have time to eat.

However, even a brief reprieve was life-giving and spirit-refreshing to Jesus, just like a short break can be for us. Immediately after Jesus attempted to withdraw from the crowds in Matthew 14, He taught thousands of men, women, and children—and then miraculously fed them all with only five loaves of bread and two fish!

Later we see the same pattern happen again: "After dismissing the crowds, he went up on the mountain by himself to pray. Well into the night, he was there alone" (v. 23).

After that, Jesus walked on the water and then met the crowds on the other side of the lake.

Living a life of simplicity isn't about breaking free from all our responsibilities; it's about being able to meet them with more power—by regularly withdrawing to spend time alone with God.

Jesus knows that a life of peace and simplicity takes effort, and He knows it may not be an easy choice for you to make in the midst of your busiest days. But He also knows that to make a significant impact on those around us, we have to intentionally make time and space to get away.

Jesus was a pro at seeking and finding His Father's presence. And if Jesus, as busy as He was, as pressured as He was to accomplish God's will in three short years, was able to get away regularly to rest, pray, and commune with God, surely He will provide a way for us to do the same. We can receive the rest and peace—and power and strength—that God offers us when we make time for Him.

What are some reasons you have for not taking time to regularly get alone, rest, and refuel your soul? Make a list here.

Now look back at the passages listed on page 21—you read at least three of them. Perhaps read the other three. How would Jesus respond to those reasons you listed above?

What do you need strength to accomplish in your daily life? How could withdrawing for a while help you?

_____

_____

_____

_____

What might God be leading you to give up or reorder in your life to make space to withdraw?

_____

_____

_____

_____

Reflect on this prayer and make it your own today:

Jesus, too often I forget that You've shown me the way to experience the power of simplicity. Sometimes I get so carried away or bogged down with life that I believe I don't have the time or ability to withdraw so that You can refuel me. Give me the courage to be more intentional about being alone with You. Give me the strength to hold fast to that boundary. Help me choose the path that leads to a simple and abundant life. Amen.

Don't be wise in your own eyes;
fear the LORD and turn away from evil.
This will be healing for your body
and strengthening for your bones.

Proverbs 3:7–8

My husband teases that I'm a hoarder. He has an ultra-minimlist outlook and says I hang on to way too many items of both clutter and sentiment. I disagree. I also choose not to count the multiple stacks of books currently on my desk as evidence that he's right.

But compared to many, our home and possessions are pretty streamlined. I don't have cabinets full of knickknacks, and I prefer cleared-off countertops and tables. But with three kids and daily deposits of school papers and junk mail, my wish isn't always my reality. Still, I think most people would characterize our material life as fairly simple.

My spiritual life, on the other hand, isn't nearly as tidy.

While I can find relief purging the junk drawer, donating unworn clothes, and throwing out all the mismatched Tupperware lids, I find it much more difficult to get rid of the unnecessary "junk" in my heart—the noise that threatens to crowd out God's voice.

I wish it weren't so. I wish I were more disciplined. I wish I had better boundaries on social media and that I never got sucked into late-night or early-morning scrolling. I long to spend as much time in God's

Word as I do messaging friends and traveling down viral video rabbit trails.

I yearn for quiet. Yet at any given time I have no less than a dozen tabs open in my internet browser. Yes, I know this slows down my system, but I like to have all the information I might need within a fingertip's click-reach. I choose this multi-tab lifestyle, yet my head spins with spreadsheets to fill out and articles to read and to-dos to check off my ever-growing list.

It's a tension I hate, but I also dread the thought of giving it up. I fear the *what-ifs*—what if I'm missing something important? Deep in my soul I desire simplicity—like I was made for it—but I'm slow to give up the complexity that masquerades as comfort and convenience.

As I face my inner frazzle, I have to admit that what I really need is more of Jesus. Oh, how I need Him. I long for quiet, for His still small voice to be louder than all the noise. Or better yet, to hush the noise of the world so that His whispers might be the single echo in my heart.

—BECKY KEIFE

Have you felt that way—that tension of wanting what the Great Shepherd has for you but being tempted by what the world offers? To have more, do more, reach for all you desire? Describe what your inner frazzle feels like.

In today's culture a lot of that pressure comes through social media. It seems so insignificant, doesn't it? Just hop online and check out what others are doing. When we measure our worth or reality against what we see on social media, however, it has a devastating effect on our happiness and our search for simplicity. A recent study out of the University of Pennsylvania found that the more time we spend on social media, the more depressed and lonely we are; it affects our mental well-being.[2]

Instead of resting in the peace and contentment that Jesus offers, we become obsessed with pursuing a filtered, fictionalized life we see online, believing if we just grasp it, it will give us the peace and contentment we long for—even though we *know* those things have been carefully crafted to present the person in a certain light.

It may not be social media cluttering your heart. Perhaps it's making sure your kids succeed, signing them up for every activity. Or maybe you constantly work overtime or serve on every committee in an effort to find worth. But those pursuits only add to our inner chaos. What we really need is much simpler—and singular: Jesus.

Proverbs 3:7–8 describes that pursuit this way: "Don't be wise in your own eyes; fear the Lord and turn away from evil. This will be healing for your body and strengthening for your bones."

A life of simplicity, a mind unfrazzled, a contented heart comes not from what the world tells us to pursue but from trusting God. When we focus on Jesus rather than on what others are doing or thinking, we find the simpler life that allows us to rest and be at peace with who we are. Inner simplicity comes when we stop seeking wisdom in our own eyes or in the eyes of others and we start seeking wisdom from the Lord.

Read Proverbs 3:1–26. Even though the author of Proverbs doesn't directly name simplicity in this passage, he does offer encouragement that can lead to a life of simplicity. Why might pursuing wisdom lead to a life of simplicity? (See vv. 13–18, for instance.)

In Proverbs 3:7, it says to "turn away from evil." We often think of evil as the really bad stuff—murder, adultery, abuse. But what if we broaden the idea to include anything that isn't good for us? With that definition in mind, how would you rate the time you spend pursuing things that appear to be good, such as social media, but leave you feeling lonely and less satisfied?

Think about the last time you spent on social media—scrolling after the kids went to bed, when waiting in the doctor's office, or while hiding in your car after picking up groceries. Or if you're filling the empty parts of your day and your heart with something else, think about that. How did you feel when you grabbed that bag of chips or put things you didn't need in your shopping cart in hopes of finding a little relief? Did it make anything simpler, or did it complicate matters? Jot down a couple words about your experience here.

Several years ago, country musician Tim McGraw sang "Live Like You Were Dying." A wise comment. The apostle Paul said something similar:

> I do want to point out, friends, that time is of the essence. There is no time to waste, so don't complicate your lives unnecessarily. Keep it simple—in marriage, grief, joy, whatever. Even in ordinary things—your daily routines of shopping, and so on. Deal as sparingly as possible with the things the world thrusts on you. This world as you see it is on its way out. (1 Cor. 7:29–31 MSG)

Live like you were dying. This world as you see it is on its way out. When we think about what we would do if we knew we didn't have a lot of time left, we discover the heart of simplicity. We cut out the white noise and seek Jesus only. We focus on loving God and loving others, finally able to let the rest of it fall away.

Life is complicated. God knows that—and He wants to take that burden from you. He wants to help you focus on what matters most. God wants to relieve your inner frazzle and replace it with His fullness and peace. So the next time you're tempted to fill a pocket of silence with scrolling, snacking, or shopping, turn to Him instead. Seek a sacred space with Him, asking how He would like you to spend your time and how you can cut out everything that clamors for your attention.

God wants to relieve your inner frazzle and replace it with His fullness and peace.

As you consider 1 Corinthians 7:29, what might keeping it simple in your daily routines look like for you?

In what ways will it take courage to practice Proverbs 3:7?

_____

_____

_____

_____

Reflect on this prayer and make it your own today:

God, I'm embarrassed and ashamed to admit that I do not live like my time is short. I often allow the world's expectations and temptations to take hold of my mind and heart. But this doesn't bring the peace that You offer. Forgive me for not seeking wisdom as I should. Help me hear Your voice. Help me listen well. And help me follow as You lead. Amen.

Come to me, all of you who are weary and burdened,
and I will give you rest.

Matthew 11:28

I sit on the edge of my bed, staring blankly at the dresser—no, *through* the dresser. My eyes are glazed over; I'm not really looking at anything. My shoulders sag, and my whole body feels as though I'm a wilting plant in need of sun and water.

I'm exhausted.

I've been saying yes to all the things that I can't say no to—family obligations, mommy duties, household upkeep, work deadlines. And then there are the yeses I say for my own well-being—therapy, life-giving friendships, time alone, church, mentoring. Throw in a celebration for someone's birthday, a coffee date with a friend I haven't seen in a while, or a visiting family member, and the calendar seems to explode at the seams, with no wiggle room even to breathe.

And running in the back of my mind is the low-humming anxiety that I'll drop a ball somewhere and won't realize it until it's too late. I can almost sense failure lurking around the corner, waiting for that ball to drop.

I close my eyes and take some deep breaths. The slow, deliberate breathing wills my body and mind to settle down. I want to curl up like a baby and be carried away to somewhere quiet so I can rest, and closing my eyes, I imagine God doing this for me. I don't have to hold or control everything so tightly when I'm held in His arms. I can relax. I can truly rest.

I lie on my bed, where I hold my palms open to my sides and close my eyes again. By habit, these verses come to mind—the words embedded into the deepest parts of me since my childhood days of memorizing Bible verses for Sunday school: "He makes me lie down in green pastures, he leads me beside quiet waters, he refreshes my soul" (Ps. 23:2–3 NIV).

Imagining the water, the green, it feels like the space I'm in expands. I don't have to be controlled by my to-do list. I don't have to do all the things or meet with all the people, even if all those things would have been good or beneficial for me.

I still need to do the things I need to do, but I look at the calendar with fresh eyes. I cancel meetings where I can. I choose only the absolutely necessary things to get done for the week. I talk with my husband about all the responsibilities I carry, and we hash out how we can better share the mental and physical loads.

In small but decisive ways, I simplify my life. And more than that, I find rest for my soul in the sliver of the day where I pause to breathe, to imagine, and to say yes to God's invitation to come and receive His rest.

—GRACE P. CHO

When was the last time you found yourself fearing failure or anxiously waiting for the ball to drop? Did you sense God's presence in that space?

Grace found some simple relief through Psalm 23, exactly where we're going today. Let's dive in a little deeper to see God's heart for us as we seek a simpler life.

> The LORD is my shepherd; I have all that I need. (Ps. 23:1 NLT)

The original word translated as "the LORD" is *Yahweh*. But Yahweh is not just a word; it's a specific name of God. In the Old Testament, a person's name was very important because it often reflected their character. So to understand why David writes that Yahweh is his shepherd, we need to understand what Yahweh means. And to do that, we need to go back to Exodus, where we find the name first used.

Read Exodus 3. In verse 14, what is the name God gives Himself?

In verse 13, Moses asks God what he should tell the Israelites when they ask who sent him. In other words, Moses wants God to provide some credibility. He is asking God, "Who are you?"

It's important for us to remember that the Israelites had been enslaved in Egypt for four hundred years, so they were very familiar with the Egyptian religion—which had one of the largest and most complex pantheons of gods and goddesses in the ancient world. The Egyptians worshiped *hundreds* of deities that each had a name and power over a particular aspect of life. For example, Isis was the goddess of fertility and motherhood. And Osiris, god of the underworld, held dominion over death, resurrection, and agricultural fertility. Each god or goddess held power only over their specific elements of life and the world.

But not the God of Israel. God tells Moses, "I AM WHO I AM." In other words, He wants His people to know that He has dominion over all things. He is self-sufficient, self-sustaining, all-powerful, eternal. The Egyptian gods and goddesses could change over time as they rose and fell in prominence, but I AM WHO I AM (the Hebrew can also be translated

"I WILL BE WHAT I WILL BE") expresses through His name that He does not change. He is secure and trustworthy. Not only that, He lets Moses know, "This is my name forever; this is how I am to be remembered in every generation" (Exod. 3:15).

God wanted Moses and the Israelites to know that He is holy, He is the great Provider, He is greatly concerned for His people, and He initiates a relationship with His people. He wanted them to understand that He is not one among many gods and goddesses. He *alone* is God. These are attributes that David knew and attested to as he wrote Psalm 23.

Read through Psalm 23 slowly. Write down the words or phrases that showcase God's attributes as listed above.

The beauty of Psalm 23, depicting our Great Shepherd, is that it is also a portal to understanding who Jesus is as Shepherd, King, and Ruler. Jesus—Immanuel, God with us—is also the great I Am. The entire Gospel of John is organized around seven "I Am" statements of Jesus.

Reflect on Jesus's "I Am" statements in the Gospel of John.

John 6:35 I Am _____.

John 8:12 I Am _____.

John 10:7 I Am _____.

John 10:11 I Am _____.

John 11:25 I Am _____.

John 14:6 I Am _____.

John 15:1 I Am _____.

It makes sense that if Yahweh is our Shepherd and will provide everything we need, then when He tells us that we can trust Him to take over our burdens, to exchange them for His way, we can trust that He has our best in mind.

By trusting the Good Shepherd, we can experience the radical simplicity of peace and contentment and courage. As the apostle Peter encourages us, "Give all your worries and cares to God, for he cares about you" (1 Pet. 5:7 NLT).

> **By trusting the Good Shepherd, we can experience the radical simplicity of peace and contentment and courage.**

What is one worry or care you can put in God's hands today? What would that look like?

_____

_____

_____

_____

Describe three of your current personal, family, and work realities. What are your greatest fears about them? In what ways do you need a fresh encounter with the Shepherd to trust that through Him you will "lack nothing"?

_____

_____

Reflect on this prayer and make it your own today:

God, I admit I've all too often allowed the familiar to become unfamiliar. I've allowed the power of Scripture to become mundane in my life. No wonder I struggle to find the peace and simple life You have for me! Give me the courage and strength to let go of what I need to so that I can embrace what You have for me. Amen.

Understand that the LORD has given you the Sabbath.

Exodus 16:29

W e were driving down the road on a Sunday afternoon when my friend began to talk about keeping
the Sabbath. I distinctly remember listening closely and
then replying, "That's great for you, and I'm glad you're
choosing Sabbath, but I just don't have time for that."

Conviction came quickly and I felt the Spirit stirring inside: *When
did checking boxes and crossing things off a list become so important
that obeying God took a back seat?*

Swept up in the current, answering every "How are you?" with "I'm
good, just busy!" I was far from rested and couldn't see an end to the
raging rapids I'd jumped into.

The following week, I decided to truly "try" Sabbath one time, to set
aside an entire day for worship and rest. It took more work than I imagined and more time to prepare than I predicted, but I was determined
to give it a shot.

It's been seven years since that afternoon drive, and choosing Sabbath has changed everything. *Everything.* And it has drawn me into a
life of simplicity I never could have imagined. It realigns my heart with
God's and reprioritizes what is most important.

When I intentionally slow down and remember my smallness in
light of God's greatness, I'm suddenly aware that I've been holding my
breath, and somehow now I can breathe again.

The addition of Sabbath is the subtraction of hurry, of rushing and performing and achieving. It's a weekly declaration to my own heart that God is more important than my to-do list. It's the recognition that when I feel I don't have time for Sabbath, I actually need it all the more.

It's a choosing and a finding, a trusting that if He breathes stars into being and walks on the water, He can surely help me handle my daily demands and concerns. I just have one requirement—to keep my eyes focused on Him.

Sabbath is an invitation to slow down and rest in God's presence, a promise made that always leads to a promise kept: He is enough.

—KAITLYN BOUCHILLON

If you practice Sabbath, how has God met you in that set-aside time to rest? If you don't practice Sabbath, what's keeping you from trying?

Of all the commandments God gave Moses on Mount Sinai, one we often break in today's fast-paced world is keeping the Sabbath.

How often have we gone about our weeks without taking a full day's rest? The reasons are easy and many: we're too busy, we don't have the time, we have too much to do. It stings to admit, doesn't it?

Yet God didn't give a command to rest because He wanted us to fall behind in our work. He gave it because He knew that without it, we'd run our striving little selves into the ground! Our Creator understands that our bodies need a break—and so do our minds and souls. We need to lie low and simply rest. But in our adrenaline-laced and overloaded world, even that can seem like work. We long for a break from the busyness without realizing that our Creator has blessed us with a rhythm for the simplicity we crave. And it's called Sabbath.

In the Old Testament book of Exodus, we see where God institutes this Sabbath and why He says it is necessary for our well-being. Let's take a look.

For hundreds of years, the Israelites had been slaves in Egypt. When they cried out for deliverance, God heard and sent Moses to break them out of their bondage. After ten plagues that grew progressively worse for the Egyptians (see Exod. 7:14–12:36), Pharaoh, Egypt's leader, released the Israelites.

They began heading toward the promised land where they would live freely. But having and keeping freedom calls for wisdom and maturity— something the Israelites lacked. For more than four hundred years they'd been told exactly what to do, how to do it, and when to do it. Every aspect of their lives had been controlled by someone else. But once they were given freedom, they didn't know how to use it wisely for their well-being. So God gave them ten instructions or boundaries to help guide and protect them—what we now call the Ten Commandments.

Read Exodus 20:1–17. Which commandments do you struggle with the most? Why?

Have you ever thought about the commandment of a Sabbath? Why do you think Sabbath is so important to God that He made it a must for us?

What do Exodus 16:23; 23:12; and 34:21 have to say about rest?

Commands might seem restrictive, but Sabbath is about freedom. God tells His people to remember the Sabbath because they had once been slaves in Egypt, never getting a day off. Similarly, today many of us find ourselves slaves to our schedules, chained to our calendars. That's why the Lord commands us to rest. He knows that, left to our own devices, we will use our freedom unwisely by filling our lives with work, doing, worry, and fear.

> **Commands might seem restrictive, but Sabbath is about freedom.**

Does practicing a weekly day of rest make you feel anxious that you won't get things done or that you'll fall behind? Are you unsure how to balance necessary care of others who rely on you with taking time to rest? Is it possible to build in time each week to prepare in advance for a day off?

Throughout history, people have taken the good of the Sabbath and turned it into another day of rules for what you are not allowed to do. But God never intended for someone else to dictate what your Sabbath should look like.

The apostle Paul clarifies this in Colossians 2:16, where he writes, "Don't let anyone judge you in regard to food and drink or in the matter of a festival or a new moon or a Sabbath day." What freedom! For your own good, God institutes a day of rest for you. Then, because He is a God of freedom, He tells you, "You rest the way you need to."

No one else can determine what resting looks like for you. As long as God is your main focus, then however you spend time resting in Him will give you strength to handle the next day (and the next and the next), for rest is ultimately not found in the absence of doing but in communing with your Creator.

It's in those ordinary, simple moments that you will begin to find the sacredness of simplicity. Sabbath rest isn't about sitting around and staring blankly at the walls. Rather, it means keeping the day simple, without obligations or pressing appointments. We aren't used to that lifestyle, are we? Our kids have practices or games. We have work responsibilities that creep into the weekends. It may feel impossible to abruptly upend your schedules—that alone can bring on tremendous stress! But you can start slow and small, asking God for wisdom to make wise and mature choices for you and your family—choices that will lead to rest.

Of every "simple" pursuit, practicing a weekly Sabbath rest may require the most courage from us as women, wives, mothers, and friends. What does Isaiah 58:13–14 promise us about courageously pursuing a Sabbath?

As you start practicing Sabbath, ask yourself, *Where have I not set boundaries? When have I said yes when I should say no?* Ask the Holy Spirit to guide you into introducing a Sabbath in your life. Listen to what He suggests. It might be by cutting one chore on that day and doing everything else normally to start. But whatever it is, determine to say yes to His leading and no where He tells you no. Write down a new Sabbath-starting idea or a boundary you know you need to set.

Reflect on this prayer and make it your own today:

God, thank You that You love me so much that You've given me the gift of rest. Give me courage to embrace it—to embrace You. Help me to keep it simple, because that's really the desire You have for me in every Sabbath. Amen.

what drives us

I am afraid that, as the serpent deceived Eve by his
craftiness, your minds will be led astray from the
simplicity and purity of devotion to Christ.

2 Corinthians 11:3 NASB

S ome old stories stick with us. That's my feeling about
the Mexican fisherman story. Maybe you've heard it?
It's a lesson about easy living—yes, about slowing down.
That we gain more of life by doing less. So I offer it here—
believing it may inspire you to uncover something true
about God's perfect pace for you too.

• • •

An American businessman watched a Mexican fisherman dock his
boat on the pier of a small coastal village. Seeing his beautiful yellowfin
tuna, the American asked how long it took to catch such wonderful
fish.

"Only a little while," the Mexican replied.

"Why don't you stay out longer and catch more?" the American
asked.

"I have enough for my family," the Mexican said.

"But what else do you do with your time?"

"Well," the fisherman said, "I sleep late, fish a little, play with my
children, take a siesta with my wife, Maria, stroll into the village each

evening where I sip wine and play guitar with my amigos. I have a full life, *señor*."

The American scoffed. "I have a Harvard MBA. You should fish more. Work more. Earn more. Buy a bigger boat—no, several boats, a fleet. Then open a cannery, move to Los Angeles, then to New York City, and run your growing enterprise."

"But, *señor*, how long will this take?"

"Oh, fifteen to twenty years," the American said.

"But what then, *señor*?"

The American laughed. "That's the best part. You would announce an IPO—initial public offering—sell your stock, and be rich. You'd make millions."

"Millions, *señor*? Then what?"

The American answered proudly, "Then you would retire, move to a small coastal fishing village, and sleep late, fish, play with your kids, take a siesta with your wife, stroll to the village in the evenings, and enjoy your friends."[1]

• • •

That's the end of this lovely story, and the point is breathtaking: working overtime to have more only leaves us with less. It isn't the lesson our world teaches, but it does line up with what Jesus says.

So, I've been trying to trim my own work pace. Focus less on the to-dos and more on being with Christ. In the process, I'm discovering how to do less for God but somehow serve Him better—enjoying Him more, and others too. Then, together, we find the simple life He promises to all—one day at a time.

—PATRICIA RAYBON

This story is really about "more," isn't it? The allure and promise of having more, which then deceives us into thinking that more will give way to a simpler life. It's a constant tension we live in. Do you feel it? How does the desire for simplicity actually compel you to strive for more?

We may long for simplicity, but we fall for the belief that we must work and struggle for the goal of *someday* to get it. We get tripped up with the world's advice that experiencing the simpler life—the life that the Mexican fisherman was already experiencing—comes by way of pursuing *more*. But for readers of the story, it's easy to see that the fisherman already had more. And as the American businessman strived for more, he actually ended up with the exact opposite. Striving for more only leaves us with less. Less of what we want, less of what we need. Less depth in our relationships, less peace, less connection with God.

This is nothing new to our day and culture. Giving away our heart and our peace in exchange for the promised "more" is a human tendency we've had since the beginning of time when Eve took that first bite of the forbidden fruit.

Let's think about Eve for a moment. This woman was the hallmark of simplicity. She lived in a perfect, stress-free garden where all her needs were met—she didn't have to worry about what to fix for dinner every night, she didn't lie awake worrying about how she and Adam were going to pay their bills, and she didn't even have closet anxiety, fretting over what she was going to wear every day or what the scale may read! And the best part was that she and God communed intimately. What could be better? What more did she possibly need to strive for?

Read Genesis 2:8–9, 15–17. What did God place in Eden that He warned Adam and Eve to stay away from?

Despite having all her needs met, Eve was tempted by the serpent who was "the most cunning of all the wild animals" (Gen. 3:1). First, he slyly twisted Eve's simple faith about God, leading her to question God's wisdom. "Did God really say, 'You can't eat from any tree in the garden'? . . . In fact, God knows that when you eat it your eyes will be opened and you will be like God, knowing good and evil" (Gen. 3:1, 5). In other words, the serpent was placing doubts in her mind about the goodness of her Creator. In essence, he was leading her to believe that God was withholding from her. If she really wanted a simple and good life, then she needed to reach for it herself.

And Eve took the bait. She began to contemplate the idea of more: "The woman saw that the tree was good for food and delightful to look at, and that it was desirable for obtaining wisdom" (Gen. 3:6). She took hold of the fruit and ate. And in that moment of reaching for more, her simple, peaceful, and good life was gone. In its place, she received shame, a broken intimacy with her Creator, a disconnected relationship with her spouse, fear and enmity with animals, pain in childbirth, loss of equality, hardship, homelessness, toil, death. Reaching for more actually gave her so much less.

Read Genesis 3. As you think about what Eve lost, in what ways have you found yourself believing those same lies of more?

The serpent suggested that God was withholding good things from Eve. But what does Psalm 84:11 tell us?

Even now, we're still tempted by distractions and deceptive promises of more. The apostle Paul tells us that focusing on Christ and finding our satisfaction in Him is the solution: "I am afraid that, as the serpent deceived Eve by his craftiness, your minds will be led astray from the simplicity and purity of devotion to Christ" (2 Cor. 11:3 NASB).

Be satisfied with the simple, and you will find the beautiful gift of more.

Be satisfied with the simple, and you will find the beautiful gift of more.

In what ways do you struggle against the enemy's craftiness in your life? How is your mind tempted to "be led astray from the simplicity and purity of devotion to Christ"?

There's an old saying, "More is less and less is more." What do you think that means? In what ways does living that way require a spiritual courage?

First John 2:15 tells us, "Do not love the world or the things in the world. If anyone loves the world, the love of the Father is not in him." What do you think the apostle means by this strong statement? What does this verse mean for how you might courageously live differently today?

Reflect on this prayer and make it your own today:

Father, I confess that too often I want the wrong kind of more. And it leads me to such dissatisfaction. Give me the strength to pursue less of this world in order to receive more of You. Amen.

Martha was distracted by her many tasks, and she came up and asked, "LORD, don't you care that my sister has left me to serve alone? So tell her to give me a hand."

Luke 10:40

I'm tired," I confess to friends over lunch one day.

"What's going on?" they ask.

"I don't really know," I say as I shrug.

That night I pull out my art journal, plug headphones into my ears, and grab a marker. I want to think through my life and especially my work. I begin to put "writer" at the top of the page, because that's my title. But as I lean toward the paper, I feel a sense of hesitation and I silently ask God, *What do you want me to write in that spot?*

I hear one word in response: *worshiper.*

Suddenly I know why I'm so exhausted. *I've switched from being a worshiper to a worker.* This isn't the first time it's happened. Through-out my life when I feel pressure mounting and expectations building, I tend to have one response: *try harder.*

Yes, I should have caught on to that pattern by now. But I'm a bit of a slow learner in this area it seems.

Maybe you have one of those areas in your life too? Thankfully, we serve a God of grace. A God who chases us down right in the middle of all our wild and weary running. A God who speaks life and peace and rest into us. A God who wants our hearts more than our hands.

I look back down at my journal and instead of writing *writer* or *worker*, I slowly spell out *w-o-r-s-h-i-p-e-r.*

A sense of peace now washes over me. Even if the world around us keeps unavoidably spinning—the toddlers keep throwing cereal, the projects keep coming, the calendar keeps filling—we can wrap our fingers around peace in a way that truly does pass understanding. And we can let go of all we've grasped that was never meant for us.

I fill the page with words and prayers. Then I set down my pen. And when I lay my head on the pillow that night, I feel different. Not so weary and afraid. Quieter inside. More like a worshiper and less like a worker.

—HOLLEY GERTH

How have you switched from being a worshiper to just being a worker?

Whether you're a full-time mom, CEO of a Fortune 500 company, part-time business employee, blossoming artist, student, or some combination of those, one thing is for sure: your life is full! If you're like most women, when someone asks how you're doing, what's typically the first thing you say? "Busy."

Though we long for simplicity, busy is our default and demands our attention. And the plates we're balancing are often good things. We honor God when we fulfill our duties at work, when we care for our family, when we engage and help others in community, when we share God's message through outreach. There is a secret, though, to leaning into the simple life in the midst of our busyness—one we see played out in the story of Mary and Martha, two sisters hosting a very important guest.

Let's read that story together.

> As Jesus and his disciples were on their way, he came to a village where a woman named Martha opened her home to him. She had a sister called Mary, who sat at the LORD's feet listening to what he said. But Martha was distracted by all the preparations that had to be made. She came to him and asked, "LORD, don't you care that my sister has left me to do the work by myself? Tell her to help me!"
>
> "Martha, Martha," the LORD answered, "you are worried and upset about many things, but few things are needed—or indeed only one. Mary has chosen what is better, and it will not be taken away from her." (Luke 10:38–42 NIV)

In what ways did Martha and Mary relate differently to Jesus?

What was Martha's gift to Jesus?

What was Mary's gift to Jesus?

Mary and Martha are some of Jesus's closest friends. The Bible specifically mentions Jesus's love for them and their brother, Lazarus (John 11:5). Martha generously opened her home to Jesus and His disciples when they were traveling and then set to work making their stay as comfortable as possible. Her hospitality revealed a kind heart and a sincere interest in the things of God. She meant to offer a true and pure gift of blessing to her guests, her friends.

But as she prepared to present her gift, she became "distracted" by the busyness, by all of her to-dos. Instead of placing her eyes on Christ to help her refocus, she placed them on her sister, Mary.

Mary would have been aware of the necessary preparations, but she chose to sit and listen to Jesus instead of helping her sister. Martha, though, struggled under the tension between enjoying her guest of honor and serving Him. If she sat there, who would get the food ready for their guests? Martha's frustration grew until, finally, she took it out on Jesus! "Lord, don't you care?"

But the rest of Martha's statement really gets to the heart of the issue: "My sister has left me to do the work by myself." Martha didn't seem to mind the preparations as much as she resented that Mary wasn't helping. Some of that frustration was probably in part because Mary didn't share Martha's priorities: get the work done first, *and then* rest and be still before Jesus.

Jesus doesn't rise to our emotional frenzy. He gently reminds us to choose what's better—Him.

Jesus responded in the most beautiful and loving way. He didn't rise to her emotional frenzy. He understood all that was on her to-do list, and He never said any of those things weren't worth pursuing. Rather, He gently reminded His dear friend about the power of refusing to allow the ever-present to-dos to distract her from the opportunity to choose what is "better"—spending time with the Lord. By saying that Mary had chosen what is better—or as some translations say, "the good"—He was also offering Martha an invitation to join them.

In what ways do you struggle with setting your priorities between the good and the better? How does this story encourage you as you prioritize both work and relationships?

Jesus told Martha that there was only one thing she needed to be concerned about. How would you describe that one thing?

_____

_____

_____

_____

Look up the following verses. In what ways do they encourage you to choose the better option of wholehearted devotion to Jesus?

Psalm 27:4–6

Psalm 42:1

Psalm 84:10

Philippians 3:7–11

_____

_____

_____

_____

_____

Reflect on this prayer and make it your own today:

Jesus, sometimes I feel consumed by work and the pressure to meet the needs in front of me. Yet I long to give my best to You—to simply be with You. Give me courage to receive the gift of Your presence, knowing that I couldn't choose anything better. Amen.

No one can serve two masters, since either he will hate one and love the other, or he will be devoted to one and despise the other. You cannot serve both God and money.

Matthew 6:24

My husband and I love attending estate auctions. We get great deals (a new leather couch for $25 and a huge box of designer handbags for $5!), and we have fun watching people bid over the oddest items (a heated toilet seat, anyone?). During one auction a few summers ago, as the bidding continued well into the sixth hour, my husband, Scott, leaned over and observed, "So much stuff. So much wasted money—and for what? To get to the end of someone's life and have it auctioned off for cents on the dollar."

Gulp.

He was right. I looked at the tables and tables of *stuff* that had been unceremoniously picked through. Some collectibles, some regular household wares, and some just trinkety junk, and I realized perhaps this auction said a whole lot more about the person than their eulogy or tombstone ever could. It spoke truth about where their heart really stood (see Matt. 6:21).

That day I began to evaluate my own "collecting" habits and what they say about me, my treasures, and my relationships. I thought about all the items I've collected over the years and have moved from shelf to drawer to shelf and from house to house. The reality check wasn't pretty: I own too much stuff. And I was forced to ask myself, *Is that really where my heart lies? With my stuff?*

Sure, I can make great excuses: I may need to use that thing at some point; it's nostalgic; it's too nice to part with; it cost a lot of money. It doesn't matter if I haven't touched it in years (decades, even). It's on hand, just in case.

But do I really need two sets of china that I never use but keep for their sentimental value? Do I really need the boxes of old smaller-sized clothes that I haven't worn since the first Gulf War (but which I'm certain I'll someday be able to slide my thighs back into)? How many coats and shoes and tea towels and screwdrivers and glasses and DVDs and spatulas and vases and books and souvenir T-shirts do I *really* need?

I went home empty-handed from that auction, but with a heart filled with determination. My life felt cluttered and unmanageable because it *was* cluttered and unmanageable. It was time to stop listening to the world that tells me I deserve to have all of this stuff—the bigger and the better. It was time to clean and clear out.

—GINGER KOLBABA

What about you? What feelings or convictions about your own stuff does this story stir up? Even if your home isn't overflowing with possessions, how much space do material things take up in your heart and mind?

When we become consumed by consumption, our lives grow complicated. Instead of our purpose being to love the Lord our God with all our heart, soul, and mind and to love our neighbor as ourselves (Matt. 22:37, 39), it becomes about accumulating things.

In and of themselves, material possessions aren't bad. First Timothy 4:4 tells us that "everything God created is good, and nothing is to be rejected if it is received with thanksgiving" (NIV). The problem is the priority we give them.

The world constantly tells us to pursue the bigger and newer and better thing. We buy an iPhone, for instance, and a year later it's outdated, so we go for the upgrade. We can become obsessed with what we have—or don't have. But all of those accumulations never quite satisfy us long-term. They promise to make our lives better, easier, simpler, but the simpler never seems to come.

The reason is that we've misplaced our sense of security. Possessions can't provide security; only God can.

Possessions can't provide security; only God can.

In His Sermon on the Mount, Jesus talked about our ultimate values, boldly challenging the ideas popularly accepted by His hearers—both then and now.

Read Matthew 6:19–24. In your own words, summarize Jesus's teaching about what your perspective should be concerning your possessions.

In what ways do you seek security through your possessions? Think of your most valued material possession. How would you feel if you lost that?

Jesus wants us to understand the temporal nature of our possessions that we house in a temporal place—where moths and rust and thieves can destroy. Solomon provided expert testimony about the fleeting nature of riches when he wrote, "Don't wear yourself out to get rich; because you know better, stop! As soon as your eyes fly to it, it disappears, for it makes wings for itself and flies like an eagle to the sky" (Prov. 23:4–5). In other words, accumulation directly opposes simplicity because it's never enough.

While as Christians we are called to live simply, our focus doesn't need to be solely on getting rid of what we have but rather on cultivating what Richard Foster calls "a joyful life of carefree unconcern for possessions."[2] That kind of outlook will lead to actions and behaviors that promote simple living.

Reread Matthew 6:24 and write it in your own words.

What does this verse mean for how you might courageously live differently today?

How can we tell if we are allowing our possessions, rather than Christ, to be our master?

Let's face it: it gets tiring having to constantly clean, manage, and organize our belongings. And for every moment we deal with our stuff, we are unable to focus on the more important aspects of a simple, God-honoring life.

Now, not everyone suffers from material excess, and selling all your stuff isn't a prescription for everyone. But this truth is for all of us: when we free ourselves from a consumptive lifestyle, we can discover the freedom of simplicity, which honors God with our trust. And opening our hands toward God, living a simpler life, and helping others along the way is exactly how we store up heavenly treasures and strengthen our spiritual connection with God.

Read Ecclesiastes 5:10–6:9. What does it say about the connection between material possessions and happiness?

Think about the last item you purchased—it could be as big as a car or as small as a cardigan. How long did it give you pleasure? How quickly did you take it for granted or wish for something newer and better?

Reflect on this prayer and make it your own today:

Father, thank You for all You have given me, for I know that all good things come from Your hands. Let me shut off my mind to the messages that tell me I should acquire more, bigger, or better. Give me courage to be satisfied with what I have. Help me remember that my security comes from You. And that is more than enough. Amen.

Don't worry, saying, "What will we eat?" or "What will we drink?" or "What will we wear?" For the Gentiles eagerly seek all these things, and your heavenly Father knows that you need them.

Matthew 6:31–32

I woke up with excruciating pain shooting in my wrists and all the way up my arms. I literally could not type one keystroke on my computer or my phone.

A trip to the doctor gave me a shocking diagnosis: I had carpal tunnel syndrome.

What? I wondered, feeling stunned. *I was fine just last night when I went to bed.*

The cause? I was working a high-profile corporate job in Silicon Valley for a maniacal boss who called me all hours of the day and night, and I didn't know how to say no. I was afraid to look for a new job because, I told myself, it was a really great opportunity career-wise and I had too many financial responsibilities. I was working demandingly long hours and my body was breaking down.

"How long will it take to heal?" I asked the doctor.

"There isn't something I can prescribe to make it go away. You're going to have to take disability and do physical therapy."

"You don't understand. I need to go back to work." I was calculating the potential damage from being away from my job. I was taking care of my mom, who was also out on disability, and I had another family member living with me. I needed the income.

I could feel the tension and anxiety building within me.

"Bonnie," the doctor said, his voice gentle and kind, "the stress from this job is not worth it. What good is a job if you can't use your hands anymore? You need to rest. Heal. Find a new job."

My doctor was encouraging me to live a simpler life. I wanted to, but could I?

I'd worked my whole life to get straight A's and put myself through college, and my try-hard life never let me down. Maybe that was the issue. It was all about me and *my* efforts. Though I'd relied on my faith to help me overcome hard times in the past, I sensed that through this health issue, God was trying to get my attention. God was asking me to lead a simpler life by doing the hardest thing I had never considered before: I needed to let go of the burdens and responsibilities I could carry no longer, and I needed to trust that He would take care of me.

I left the doctor's office knowing it was time to make a decision—a simple one, really, but oh so difficult. I needed to quit my job and look for a new one. One that would respect the simpler life God was calling me to. I needed to admit my limitations and stop letting this job take over my life and my worries. I had to trust that through what I perceived to be a risky, scary, radical action, God would be there, holding me and allowing me to experience the simplicity that my soul longed for. It was time to let go of a job where I depended on my productivity and accomplishments to provide for my family. It was time to simply trust and embrace the simplicity of my faith that calls me to depend on God.

—BONNIE GRAY

How have you depended on your own effort, productivity, or accomplishments?

It's difficult to let go of the things that seem so sure—even when they're complicated and unhealthy—in order to cling to the risky, scary, and radical ways of Jesus, isn't it? And yet, this is exactly God's heart for you as a courageous woman of simplicity.

In the Sermon on the Mount, Jesus shows us how and why we need to hold loosely to our possessions. As we continue to look at this sermon in Matthew 6:25–33, we see that Jesus shows us what we'll find when we let go of those concerns for possessions: freedom from worry.

Let's look at the passage. Jesus starts with an important word: *therefore.*

Immediately before He tells us not to worry, Jesus explains that clinging tightly to things on earth—rather than storing up treasures in heaven—will destroy who we are. He then makes the bold claim that we cannot serve both God and money (or possessions). Though He's asking us to choose between Him and earthly wealth, He also says that if we choose Him, we will never have to worry about our life again. That's a hefty promise!

Look up Matthew 6:25–33 and read it. What "proof" does Jesus present to showcase that God is trustworthy?

Notice how often in those few verses Jesus repeats that you should not worry—four times! What does that tell you about God's concern and care for you?

Why do you think Jesus emphasizes that you shouldn't be worried or anxious about your daily life? What is the simple antidote to help us not worry (see v. 33 in particular)?

Faster than almost anything, worry can crowd out our ability to trust. That is why Jesus teaches us to seek the ways of His kingdom first—that we remember God's power and faithfulness. Only when we focus our eyes, hearts, and minds on God and the things of God will we be able to respond well to the crises or potential crises that appear in our lives. Worst-case scenarios no longer play havoc with our minds as we remember that God is bigger than our fears.

Only when we trust God to provide for us will we break free of anxiety and fear and worry. As we see God's faithfulness in each circumstance, we will build our trust muscles. As we trust more, our faith will grow. And as our faith grows, it will squeeze out those remnants of worry. Romans 12:2 tells us, "Do not be conformed to this age, but be transformed by the renewing of your mind, so that you may discern what is the good, pleasing, and perfect will of God."

As we renew our minds, trusting God to handle our lives, we are able to remain calm in the midst of the world's fears and worries—we experience simplicity in the midst of life's chaos. We are invited to live a life of pure and simple devotion to Christ.

As you consider seeking first God's kingdom and renewing your mind, what might that look like for you in your everyday life and relationships?

God wants more for you. When your mind is filled with anxiety, you can't possibly find simplicity. But when you take captive every thought to make it obedient to Christ, as 2 Corinthians 10:5 says, you will experience the deeply satisfying and enduring peace of Christ.

When your mind is filled with anxiety, you can't possibly find simplicity.

Look up the following passages. What is the promise or reward in each? Write your observations on what these encouragements mean to you.

Psalm 55:22

Nahum 1:7

Philippians 4:6–7

1 Peter 5:7

How do we stop worrying? By focusing on the truths of God. Think about a time in which you chose not to worry and instead focused on God's truths. Write it here and then write what happened. How did you feel? In what way did you experience God's faithfulness to you through it?

Write out Matthew 6:31–32 in your own words—and add your name in the text, as though Jesus is speaking directly to you.

What does this verse mean for how you might courageously live differently today?

Reflect on this prayer and make it your own today:

God, I need courage to remove worry from my mind. I don't want dark or anxious thoughts to control me and send my mind in every direction apart from trusting You. Thank You that You care about me and my needs. You are a good, good Father. Amen.

A pretentious, showy life is an empty life;
a plain and simple life is a full life.

Proverbs 13:7 MSG

Growing up, I had never heard of a "stay-at-home mom" (SAHM). In my community, everyone worked somewhere outside of the home. As a child, I believed that the few people in my community who did not "go to work" were retired, disabled, or between jobs. Having a job was the norm and was equated with status, merit, and value.

You know the standard prompt asked of children: "What do you want to be when you grow up?" As children, we knew the drill. We must reply with a position or title deemed an economically valuable and worthwhile contribution to the community. As a child, I learned to answer, "Lawyer." Other acceptable answers would have been business owner, doctor, nurse, banker, or even president of the United States! But never in my entire young life was SAHM even a concept, let alone an option.

While teaching undergraduates at a university far away from my childhood community, I was dumbfounded each time I heard one of my students say that she wanted to be a SAHM. I didn't know that SAHM could be an aspiration, even a notable one. I trekked along on my planned path of charting research goals, meeting publishing quotas, and planning my contributions to the world.

A few years later, newly married and relocated, I found myself, for the first time, without a job. With no position or even a clue of what to do next, I felt worthless. I had found my value in being a hard worker and a high achiever. I was embarrassed not to be working. And folks from my childhood community did not hesitate to express their disappointment in me. "Why would you go to school for all those years and then not work? You are wasting your degrees!" I heard this over and over from "well-meaning" friends and family.

Facing disappointment—theirs and mine—was excruciating. It took years, but I learned to walk in the peace of simply being—knowing my worth and knowing I am valuable and can have a full life because I exist, not because of what I do.

So after I had my first baby, when the pediatrician asked me, "Will you be going back to work or staying home with her?" for the first time I was overwhelmed with peace about being a SAHM. This option, which I had not deemed acceptable, offered a type of courageous simplicity I needed during that season of our lives. I realized that being a working mom wasn't somehow better than being a SAHM or vice versa, and over the years I've had the privilege of being whatever works best for our family. What I did find, however, was that I needed to embrace a courageous simplicity based on what my family and I needed and what we felt God calling us to. And as I've listened and pursued it, I've received a simple but wonderfully fulfilling life.

—LUCRETIA BERRY

Do you wrestle with believing your worth is based on what you do rather than simply being who you are? Describe this feeling.

Is there anyone who doesn't want a full and meaningful life? We'd be hard-pressed to find someone. Yet when we suggest that embracing simplicity is the means to fulfillment, cue the sighs and rolling eyes, because many believe simplicity is just not realistic.

But the truth may be that we struggle with the courage to embrace simplicity. Perhaps, like Lucretia discovered, we wrestle with our own misconceptions or what others might think if we pursue a simpler life. Perhaps we avoid true simplicity because it threatens to strip us of our appearance of control. Perhaps it promises to show who we are under all our posturing and positioning, our makeovers and renovations, our organized pantries and impressive social media platforms, our well-ordered social calendars and family achievements. Perhaps we avoid it because living the simple life means we must give up some of our ideals about how we want others to view us or even how we determine our own value. In other words, perhaps we avoid simplicity because it begins by eroding our pride.

Today, let's turn our eyes again to Jesus's friends Mary and Martha.

Read John 12:1–8. In what way did Mary courageously step forward and abandon her pride?

On their way to Jerusalem, Jesus and His disciples again came back through Bethany where Mary and Martha lived. Mary, unconcerned with how others perceived her and fully abandoned to God, brought expensive perfume and poured it on Jesus's feet, then wiped them with her hair. The Gospels of Matthew and Mark also describe the scene but say that she anointed His head (Matt. 26:7; Mark 14:3). Perhaps she anointed both, starting with His head and finishing with His feet.

It was common courtesy in that time to wash a guest's feet, but it was unusual to anoint them with such expensive perfume. And then Mary wiped Jesus's feet *with her hair*. This extraordinary act showed Mary's genuine humility in the presence of Jesus. Her compelling desire to worship Him, minister to Him, and show her overwhelming love for Him clearly overrode any embarrassment or pride. She didn't care about the cost of the perfume; she didn't care about all the eyes on her; she didn't care about what others thought or said. She had a singular, simple focus: Jesus and only Jesus.

Whatever you do in life, what ultimately matters is Jesus. As Proverbs 13:7 reminds us, "A pretentious, showy life is an empty life; a plain and simple life is a full life" (MSG).

Mary and Martha had a full life. You can have one too. When we focus on Jesus, our simple tasks become extraordinary offerings. If we dwell too much on what others think, or on the sacrifice or plainness of something, we might get cold feet or become discouraged or unmotivated to do it. But when we remember the One to whom we offer our simple abandonment—giving our all to the One who gave His all—we won't second-guess our decisions for Jesus. Our simple devotion to Him will simply grow. Others may call our decisions careless, foolish, even dangerous, but their opinions are irrelevant. Jesus's approval is all that matters.

> **When we focus on Jesus, our simple tasks become extraordinary offerings.**

As you consider Proverbs 13:7 (see above), in what ways do you need courage to live a less pretentious, showy life—or let go of your need for approval from others—and embrace a plain and simple life?

_____

_____

Mary abandoned her pride. *Abandon* means to yield yourself fully and without restraint, to relinquish, to surrender. Abandoning our pride births freedom and simplicity. Choose two or three of the following passages (or all of them if you are really feeling industrious!) and answer this question: How does Scripture encourage you to abandon your life to God?

Mark 8:34–37   Ephesians 4:22–24

Romans 8:1–4   Philippians 2:5–8

Galatians 2:20

_____

_____

_____

_____

_____

_____

Reflect on this prayer and make it your own today:

Lord God, I have much to learn about abandoning my life to You, surrendering my will to Yours. I still struggle against my pride and what others may think and say about me. How I long to do as Mary did, though—to worship You wholeheartedly and live in simplicity with my focus on You. Grant me that strength and courage, I pray. Amen.

living in the sacred present

What you're doing is not good. . . . You will certainly
wear out both yourself and these people who are with
you, because the task is too heavy for you. You can't do
it alone.

Exodus 18:17–18

Too often I find my worth in doing things for people, in being needed. When the email comes in that the foster family we support is in need of diapers or food, I email them back and ask, "What kind?" or "Anything you'd like to eat tonight?" When my sister-in-law's family of six is sick with the stomach bug, I offer to cook them rice porridge as comfort food. When a friend is in crisis, I'm quick to drop everything to meet her for coffee and a chat.

And when I get lost in being there for others at every turn, I come out the other side feeling haggard. My temper is short, my patience lost. I'm snappy and overly sarcastic, and my tone is jagged, cutting my words into sharp edges that hurt those closest to me even when I don't intend to.

Unfortunately, when I'm burned out from helping others so that I can feel needed and important, my family bears the brunt of the worst of me. Instead of being first on my list of priorities, they get pushed down to last, and instead of being present with them, I'm absent while being present for everyone else.

Searching for my significance by what I can do for others is like running on a hamster wheel—I can run as hard as I want, but I'll get nothing out of it except an emptier, hungrier soul. And it's not just me that hurts from it afterward, but my kids and my marriage hurt as well.

Recently, my kids shared how they wished I were better at playing LEGOs with them. They said it matter-of-factly, a simple request for their mom to really be with them, engaged in the holy work of play. I thought what I deserved was praise from others about how well I could fill their needs, but what I learned was that my family deserves to get all of me, here and now.

I can't add to or take away from my worth by what I do to meet everyone else's needs. I am already significant, and from that place I can rest, sit on the floor, and play LEGOs with my kids.

—GRACE P. CHO

Have you ever struggled with that hamster-on-the-wheel feeling—doing for others to the point that you feel haggard? Describe what happens to you when you serve others at the expense of your own family or your relationship with the Lord.

We know that too much of a good thing can be bad, but it might be surprising to realize this includes serving others. Our default setting seems to be stuck on giving away all we have to our spouse and children and neighbors and coworkers and . . . and . . . and . . . And we see the value in serving—after all, that's what God has called us to. As Hebrews 13:16 encourages us, "Do not forget to do good and to share with others, for with such sacrifices God is pleased" (NIV).

The problem we often struggle with is finding the balance between serving others and allowing ourselves time to refuel. Instead we continue to go full steam ahead, only stopping when our reserves are depleted and we're forced to, such as when we find ourselves stuck in bed with the flu. And, as Grace's story illustrates, sometimes we confuse serving out of the strength God gives us with serving to find our worth.

> **Sometimes we confuse serving out of the strength God gives us with serving to find our worth.**

Ultimately, perhaps it comes down to our confusion: we've mistaken nonstop service to others with pleasing God. So why don't we feel at peace? Let's be clear— service to others *does* please God, as we've seen in the above verse from Hebrews. But God is also very concerned with meeting our needs as well.

In what ways have you confused serving others with pleasing God?

Look up Mark 12:30–31. In the second great command, which we read here, what does Jesus assume about loving our neighbor? Do you believe that it's okay to love yourself as God does? Why or why not?

Moses understood this idea of trying to care for everyone. He had more than six hundred thousand men, plus women and children (that's upwards of two to three million total) he felt responsible for (see Exod. 12:37). That's a lot of pressure!

Let's look together at what happened when he tried to serve all of them by himself.

Problems! Nothing but problems! This must have been what Moses thought as he guided the Israelites through the wilderness. After the excitement and enthusiasm of their miraculous freedom wore off, the Israelites erupted into questions and disputes over how to handle their new lives. They needed guidance over everyday matters and didn't have the Ten Commandments yet, so they looked to Moses, their leader, to rule on a multitude of daily disagreements. Exodus 18:13 tells us that "Moses sat down to judge the people, and they stood around Moses from morning until evening."

Imagine trying to meet people's needs and fix their predicaments from dawn to dusk every day—over and over and over. (Maybe imagining isn't hard because you know this pressure too.) It's exhausting just to think about! Moses must have been overwhelmed, drained, fatigued, and more than a little frustrated and grumpy, right?

Fortunately, Moses received a visit from his father-in-law, Jethro, who brought along Moses's wife and sons. Moses told Jethro about all the good things God had done, and they rejoiced over it all (Exod. 18:7–12). Moses was serving the Lord! It was all good, right?

Undoubtedly Moses wanted to spend more time visiting with his wife and family—but he couldn't, because his schedule was too demanding. The next day, as Moses was busily caring for everyone's needs, Jethro saw and lovingly confronted him.

Read Exodus 18:13–26 and answer the following questions:

What did Jethro say to Moses (in particular vv. 14 and 17)?

What did Jethro say would be Moses's reward for following his advice (see v. 23)?

_____

_____

_____

How did Moses respond (vv. 24–26)?

_____

_____

_____

How might Jethro's insight and wisdom and Moses's response apply to your experience?

_____

_____

_____

Think about the people in your life. To whom could you delegate work or responsibilities? What might that delegation look like? What's keeping you from reaching out to them?

_____

_____

_____

Moses saw the wisdom of his father-in-law's words and applied them. He delegated—something we should try to do as we seek the simplicity of focusing on the most important needs, including our own.

The apostles also learned the importance and power of delegation. Read Acts 6:1–7. Write what was happening and what was causing issues for the apostles. What was their response? How did it work out?

Reflect on this prayer and make it your own today:

Father, I love to help others when I can. I know it pleases You too. But I tend to take on too much and forget to take care of myself. Remind me that You live in me—and that what I do or don't do reflects on You. Give me wisdom to know when I need to delegate and how to receive a greater measure of Your strength. Amen.

Why, my soul, are you so dejected?
Why are you in such turmoil?
Put your hope in God, for I will still praise him,
my Savior and my God.

Psalm 43:5

I was in the twilight zone. That was the only rationale keeping me afloat during the first year of my marriage. I had married one of my closest friends. Before the wedding, I admired and respected him so much. But when the honeymoon was over, the honeymoon was over.

My marriage felt like a cruel joke. All the certainty of soaring into a bright future with my husband seemed to fall flat into impossibility. I felt as though God had chosen my husband over me; his dreams and plans automatically voided mine.

As our two lives morphed into one, our new life seemed a sole reflection of my husband. I felt forgotten, overlooked, and undervalued.

"God," I prayed, "why did You give me dreams, visions, and desires only to experience the disappointment of not having them realized?" Brokenhearted and full of resentment, I eventually gave up. I decided to let go of the life I'd glimpsed through prayer. I could no longer do the mental tug-of-war. Even if it meant I'd live someone else's life, at least I'd live it in peace.

So I let go. I surrendered. I stopped working so hard to convince God that I was smart, talented, and worthy of the abundant life that stirred within me—the life that had been replaced by my husband's life. I stopped trying to build my spiritual résumé. I stopped striving for value. I stopped.

And once I stopped, once I stood still and began to simply live, I began to see God's dreams for me manifesting through the life I shared with my husband. I learned to keep my focus in the present instead of worrying about the future. Since then, I've watched my life align with God's design for me in oneness with my husband. I did not need to wrestle for it or shout for it. I only needed to be still and know who God is.

—LUCRETIA BERRY

Is there a time when you struggled with letting go of your dreams or when life hasn't worked out the way you planned? Or maybe you're feeling that now. Write briefly about it here.

A woman in the Old Testament struggled with dreams lost and pain realized. Though her name means "pleasant," Naomi was far from it— and for good reason. A famine had struck the land of Judah. So Elimelech packed up his wife, Naomi, and his two sons, Mahlon and Chilion, and traveled to Moab to wait out the famine. While they were there, the sons both married pagan (non-Jewish) women and began to make lives for themselves. But tragedy soon struck.

Elimelech died. And then Mahlon and Chilion died. The Bible simply states, "Naomi was left without her two children and without her husband" (Ruth 1:5). But there's a world of hurt if you read between the lines. Naomi was now a foreigner, a widow, and alone. All she had left were two daughters-in-law to provide for. Plus, being a woman in ancient times bore its own challenges, as women weren't treated as equal to men and were generally forbidden from things like owning land. There is certainly nothing that provides the simplicity of a peaceful, tranquil life in this story line.

What's even more painful is the explanation Naomi gave for her suffering: "The LORD's hand has turned against me" (Ruth 1:13). Rather than seeing God's hand as a gentle, loving, guiding presence in her life, she saw it as a slap in her face—cruel, withholding.

Read Ruth 1. How did Naomi's troubles affect her faith? How might such a tragedy affect your faith?

After Naomi returned to Bethlehem, her homeland, the Bible says, "The whole town was stirred" and the women asked, "Is this Naomi?" (v. 19 ESV). What do you think they were really asking?

How did Naomi greet the townspeople (see v. 20)?

It's a guarantee that troubles and trials will show up in our lives. Some are relatively minor—we fracture an ankle when we slip and fall on some ice, or we lose the promotion we were promised. Some are more catastrophic—we are diagnosed with a disease, our house burns down, someone steals our identity, or our best friend dies suddenly. No matter how great or small, every trial we face is an opportunity to respond with steadfast simplicity. Adversity should never come as a surprise—Jesus told us that we will experience suffering and trouble as long as we live.

Read John 16:33. What does Jesus tell us to do? Why?

Choosing to embrace simplicity—that single-minded focus on following the Lord—will equip us and give us the strength to remain resolute in the midst of any circumstance. That doesn't mean we won't still feel the weight of the trouble or trial, but we cling to the God who is bigger and stronger than the circumstance. Look up the following verses. What do they tell us about why we can be strong and courageous in the midst of troubles?

    Joshua 10:25
    Matthew 7:24–27
    John 10:27–30
    Romans 8:35–39

James 1:2–8 and 1 Peter 1:3–9 encourage us to rejoice in our trials. Reflect below on why the Lord wants you to rejoice when you face difficult circumstances.

Is there bitterness toward God that you've held onto because of something you felt He should have done but didn't? In what ways has that bitterness kept you from a sense of peace?

Let's go back to our friend Naomi. Something interesting happens with Naomi as we travel through the book of Ruth. It's clear that something changes within her—something very good. She begins to praise God rather than blame Him.

When her daughter-in-law Ruth reported to her all about the kindness a man named Boaz had shown, Naomi said, "May the LORD bless him!" (Ruth 2:20 NLT). Her tone sounds very different, doesn't it? Had her grief gone away? Was her tragedy no longer tragic? No. But her perspective was changing. Naomi was offering a sacrifice of praise (see

Heb. 13:15). Praising God in the midst of good times is easy; praising Him when hardship comes costs us something—but we still praise because God is still good. He doesn't change just because our circumstances do.

> **Sometimes the simple comes through fighting hard, being doggedly determined, offering a sacrifice of praise.**

A life of simplicity seldom comes easily. Sometimes the simple comes through fighting hard, being doggedly determined, offering a sacrifice of praise. Ecclesiastes 7:14 reminds us, "In the day of prosperity be joyful, but in the day of adversity, consider: God has made the one as well as the other." When we learn to embrace them both, we will discover an unshakable simplicity and peace.

Reflect on a dark time when God called you to offer a sacrifice of praise. Did you? If not, what kept you from it?

In what ways would you say praising God in the middle of a trial takes courage? In what ways does it also bring simplicity into our lives?

How you respond to adversity affects your ability to live a peaceful life, a courageous life. Responding incorrectly can actually end up compounding your anguish. Ask the Holy Spirit to bring to mind how

you handle those difficult times and in what ways He is calling you to be brave and choose differently. Write the insights and wisdom He gives you.

Reflect on this prayer and make it your own today:

Father, protect me from feeling bitter toward You or believing that You cause bad things to happen. When troubles come my way, let my soul determine to praise You and let my mind remember that You are good and faithful and kind—always. Amen.

Wait for the LORD;
be strong, and let your heart be courageous.
Wait for the LORD.

Psalm 27:14

*D*well.

That's what the Holy Spirit whispered to my heart.

I thought God would be telling me to unpack my boxes, get settled in my house, or prepare for the next thing He wanted us to do here. But instead He said, "Dwell."

The word *dwell* sounded almost lazy. What good does dwell do? What does dwell do at all?

God had been teaching me about a promised land that He offers all of those who love Him. It was a new concept for me to understand the idea of what He spends most of the Old Testament trying to teach us. He had guided our family to purchase ten acres, burn down the existing home, and build a modern farmhouse. We thought it was for us to share with our family and friends, grow and sell food, and host events. We had aspiring plans and loads of ideas for our new home.

The years before beginning life in our promised land had been difficult. My husband traveled extensively with his job, so I was by myself, raising our baby turning toddler who didn't sleep much, and I felt very alone.

I was beyond exhausted. But the Lord was gracious. He brought us to a special place and asked us to dwell. To wait on Him and to enjoy

Him and all He had done on our behalf. To abide in Him. To take time to see Him and His work and to praise His name.

God asked us not to run on to the next thing with a winded hallelujah but to enjoy Him in the place He called us and gave to us.

I learned during those quiet moments of dwelling that being tucked inside God because we're tuckered out is one of the purest forms of love the Father tries to show us. God doesn't ask more from us but less, so He can pour in His love into the worn-out places of our souls and refresh our spirits.

I learned I had to keep things simple, not do as much as I wanted or what I thought others could accomplish in my situation, and simply listen and obey the voice of God. Only then could I be still long enough to dwell.

—STEPHANIE BRYANT

Can you think of a time when God asked you simply to dwell? What did that season look like for you? What did you learn about God? About yourself?

Dwell. In many ways, *dwell* is another word for *wait*. Over and over the Bible tells us to wait on or for the Lord. In our humanness, we want to rush ahead, accomplish our goals, take care of business. We don't like to wait. It doesn't feel productive, and that doesn't sit well with us.

The world doesn't like to wait. Think about the aggravation you have seen in others who have to wait—or even in yourself. Waiting in a long line with a slow cashier. Being put on hold when making a phone call. Sitting in a waiting room at a doctor's office as the clock ticks past your scheduled appointment time. It's tiresome, a waste of time. We prefer action and productivity!

We tend to see waiting as a delay, a detour on our schedules. We see it as a barren or passive season of life we must endure, believing God is silent or withholding from us. We believe the best we can hope for is that it will soon be over—but in the meantime, we think, *Ugh. Let's get on with it! God, where* are *You? Why aren't You* doing *something?*

> Living a life of simplicity invites us to see waiting not as something to be endured but as something sacred to be enjoyed.

Living a life of simplicity, however, invites us to see waiting not as something to be endured but as something sacred to be enjoyed. Waiting isn't passive or unproductive. With a simplicity mindset, we understand that in waiting, something is happening, the Lord is working. Waiting then becomes an essential part of pursuing a simple and pure devotion to Christ, an active exercise of faith.

Have you ever thought about waiting as a way of life rather than a means of trying to get through a particular season? How might this change in perspective alter your mindset?

Consider Isaiah 40:31: "They who wait for the Lᴏʀᴅ shall renew their strength; they shall mount up with wings like eagles; they shall run

and not be weary; they shall walk and not faint" (ESV). What gifts are described here? Who receives them?

_____

_____

_____

_____

When we wait for the Lord, in a sense we are waiting "for the LORD's help" (NET). In other words, we are waiting for some kind of rescue or assistance. Other Bible translations refer to it as waiting on the Lord (NKJV), trusting in the Lord (CSB, NLT), and hoping in the Lord (NIV). From these different translations we can see that waiting, trusting, and hoping are all biblically connected.

Waiting on the Lord is the key to receiving renewed strength along with a deeper understanding of and relationship with God. It then becomes a privilege, a spiritual pleasure to wait.

Read Isaiah 33:2–6. In what ways were the people waiting on and waiting for the Lord?

_____

_____

_____

_____

What are some things you are waiting for? In what ways might you consider the wait a privilege if you thought about it as an opportunity to worship?

Waiting on the Lord is not only about faith but also about obedience. So how do we learn to wait in a way that pleases God and strengthens our simple devotion to Him? We spend time listening to Him speak to us through His Word, through our prayers, and by meditating on the things of God's kingdom.

Waiting isn't easy—it isn't meant to be. But waiting on God as a way of everyday living will lead us into a deeper relationship that offers us the peace and promise of a simple life.

Go to Biblegateway.com, use a Bible app, or grab a concordance and look up the phrases "wait on the Lord," "wait for the Lord," "hope in the Lord," and "trust in the Lord." Choose at least three verses that come up in your search and write those here to remind yourself of the power and promise that come with this attitude of waiting.

In what ways does viewing waiting as a spiritual lifestyle take courage? Why?

_____

_____

_____

_____

Reflect on this prayer and make it your own today:

Lord, I don't wait well. I'm too impatient. But I know that waiting isn't just about wanting something to happen. It's ultimately about worshiping You and trusting that You've got everything handled, that You are worthy of my trust. Help me to remember that You aren't passive; You are actively working on my behalf! Let me glorify You and be obedient to You as I wait. Amen.

Blessed are the poor in spirit,
for the kingdom of heaven is theirs.

Matthew 5:3

Born to a teenage mom and a dad who left when I was seven, I grew up poor. I aspired to change this fact and create a better life for myself and my family. I also wanted to grow up to be an encourager, serving God and others.

Despite my hardships at home, I grew up in a wonderful church life, where faith was reflected in Sunday school teachers teaching, worship leaders singing, and missionaries changing lives. Serving in ministry and loving on others was how I felt I belonged, how I could be seen and valued.

I did grow up to become a missionary, Bible teacher, and ministry leader, but when I started to experience panic attacks after becoming a mom of two boys, I suddenly lost my ability to do even simple things, such as trying to breathe and get through the day, because I was exhausted from insomnia. The moment I realized I had to stop serving was the scariest moment.

Who would I be if I couldn't serve and encourage others? What would I do now? Even the simplest things began to overwhelm me. One day I stood in the supermarket aisle and cried because I couldn't decide which herbal tea to buy. I couldn't drink coffee anymore because caffeine was exacerbating my body's stress. It seemed pitiful that a "good day" was now reduced to drinking tea and getting out of bed. Taking a walk became the highlight of my day.

But I learned something on my journey of healing from anxiety: when I had nothing to give, God met me deeply in this simple life of taking walks and learning to restore God's peace to my body and soul. This poverty of spirit opened the doorway to emotional intimacy, because in those walks I experienced God's deep comfort. I found this simplicity of life allowed me to slow down and spend time with people doing simple things, like inviting others over for tea and a walk. And during those times, I found people opening up to me so much more deeply because I wasn't asking for anything in return. I was just focused on spending time together, not on busyness and serving. I had no agenda other than sharing what gave me peace and joy and enjoying their company.

I learned that I am blessed because I am poor in spirit, because I return to simply being God's beloved. The world becomes a more beautiful place of God's refuge, joy, and peace. This poverty of spirit is really the gift of simplicity.

—BONNIE GRAY

Have you ever experienced a time when you lost the ability to do even simple things? What happened? What was that like for you?

Jesus talked about having that impoverished spirit Bonnie refers to above. Though she initially saw it as a detriment, she learned to see it through a different lens. Did it change her circumstances? No, but it did change her attitude and her ability to rejoice and praise God through her difficulties.

Though Jesus didn't use the word *simplicity*, He had much to say about this single-minded devotion to God. Let's look together at one of His most well-known sayings. We find it in His Sermon on the Mount.

Jesus had traveled throughout Galilee healing people of all kinds of physical diseases. With the Sermon on the Mount, Jesus addressed the inner workings of a person's life. The outer healed body is of little value if the inner body remains sick. So He focused—as was the principal purpose of His ministry—on the soul's condition. During that sermon He presented the Beatitudes, or what we might call the "beautiful attitudes": mindsets to grow inside of us that lead us into a God-honoring life. He wants us to understand that by embracing these attitudes, which guided the way Jesus Himself acted and reacted, we can live a happy and victorious life—a "blessed" life.

If you have time, read all of Matthew 5 to see more of the attitudes Jesus wants us to embrace, but for today's study, we're going to focus on one particular beautiful attitude: simplicity.

Read Matthew 5:1–12. Which of the Beatitudes does Jesus discuss first? Write it here.

Why do you think Jesus lists this beatitude first?

What do you think Jesus meant by being "poor in spirit"?

A person who is poor isn't inferior to other people but instead is emptied and in need. The Greek word translated in verse 3 as "poor" is a word used to describe the poorest of the poor. Jesus isn't saying that someone who is poor in spirit is a poor-spirited person but instead is someone who realizes she doesn't have her spiritual life all together. She realizes she needs help. And she understands that help comes first from God and then from God's people. A person who is poor in spirit is a humble person. She is willing to learn more about God and His ways. Being poor in spirit means we simplify our devotion, our focus, to one thing: God. Everything becomes about Him. And all our behaviors flow from taking on the mindset of simplicity.

Describe what a humble person looks like. How do you know someone is humble?

In Matthew 6:21, Jesus says, "Where your treasure is, there your heart will be also." In what ways might this relate to being poor in spirit? Explain.

The beautiful aspect to all of these attitudes is that we receive something wonderful in return. God, who is the Giver of every good and perfect gift (see James 1:17), lavishes His blessings upon us. And each specific godly attitude we embrace comes with its own reward.

Reread Matthew 5:3. What is the reward God gives us for embracing a pure and simple devotion to Him?

The promise of the kingdom of heaven is a reward we receive both in this present life and in the eternal life to come. For the present life, experiencing the kingdom of heaven means that we are led by God. When we empty ourselves, He fills us. And in that filling we go from being poor to receiving heaven's wealth!

The arrogant person won't admit she needs God or others. But the poor in spirit depend on God—and they are buoyed up.

> **When we empty ourselves, He fills us. And in that filling we go from being poor to receiving heaven's wealth!**

We admit that we own nothing that would make us worthy of salvation, that we have no way of earning God's favor, and that we owe a sin debt we cannot pay. We come to Jesus on those terms and we receive all the rights and privileges and benefits of a child of God!

Would you consider yourself poor in spirit? Why or why not?

In what ways does being poor in spirit require courage?

_____

_____

_____

By embracing this beautiful attitude, how might you live differently today?

_____

_____

_____

Reflect on this prayer and make it your own today:

Father, I long to become more like Christ. Empty me of everything but Him, so that You can fill me with the things of Your kingdom. Amen.

Be still, and know that I am God.

Psalm 46:10 ESV

I was excited but stressed. I had a list I needed to get done and not enough time to do it. But it was Saturday, the day I told Jesus I would set aside to Sabbath.

I don't Sabbath in a legalistic way—or at least, I try not to. Instead, I frame my day around four ideas: stop, rest, delight, and worship. Typically one leads into the next—stopping moves me to resting, resting transports me to delighting in the world around me, and delighting causes worship to spring forth from my heart and lips.

My Sabbaths ultimately lead me into trusting—knowing God has everything taken care of. I'm not in control. The world will keep turning without me. And that's okay.

But on this Saturday, I began my Sabbath frayed, wondering if I could cheat to get my to-do list done.

I splayed my Bible open on the coffee table, hoping to calm my anxious heart. Then I glanced up and read the sign on my wall. It's directly in front of the couch where I meet God in the mornings. It's technically Christmas decor, but I've yet to take it down because I need the words each day.

Be still and know that I am God.

A simple life is an unhurried life. I used to think that busy was best and that hustle meant I was important, but the longer I get to know Jesus, the more I see how slow and thoughtful His approach to living was. And it's not as though Jesus didn't have a lot to do.

Be still and know . . .

I took a deep breath. I didn't want to cave in to the pressure of hustle culture and once again become addicted to hurry. I pushed my to-do list away from my mind and leaned into the peace and stillness of God. I closed my eyes and breathed. I pictured Jesus, a non-anxious presence—the opposite of hustle and hurry.

I chose to be still. In my choice, I realized: He is God and I am not. He's holding everything together. I couldn't even if I tried.

I can stop and rest, and the God of the universe will keep the world spinning without my help—and that is a good, beautiful thing indeed.

—ALIZA LATTA

How often have you thought of that well-known verse to be still and know that He is God and then continued on with life at the same pace? Why do you think it is so easy to read something but not allow the words to penetrate your spirit, heart, and mind?

Psalm 46:10 is a powerful verse for us: "Be still, and know that I am God" (ESV). *The Message* paraphrase says, "Step out of the traffic!" Other translations tell us to "calm down" (CEV), "stop your fighting" (CSB), "let go of your concerns" (NOG), "cease striving" (NASB), and "surrender your anxiety" (TPT). We may say, "Relax!" But this relaxing isn't about physical stillness, although that certainly is appropriate; it's about heart stillness.

But even that is only the first part of the instruction. Ceasing alone will not provide the simplicity of heart and soul we ultimately desire.

It's what we do in and with the stillness that matters: we are to *know* that He is God.

How can we be still when the world around us is frenzied and our to-do lists are overwhelming? We focus on who God is.

It's interesting that the psalmist doesn't start with the directive and then prove its worth by establishing who God is. The psalmist starts with God— exactly where our simple and pure devotion calls us to start.

> **Ceasing alone will not provide the simplicity of heart and soul we ultimately desire. It's what we do in and with the stillness that matters.**

Read Psalm 46 slowly out loud. It is said that whenever Martin Luther would hear discouraging news, he'd say, "Come, let us sing the forty-sixth psalm."[1] In fact, Luther was so moved by this psalm, he based his hymn "A Mighty Fortress Is Our God" on it.[2] What do you think it is about Psalm 46 that made Luther claim it in the midst of discouragement?

The psalmist wants us to understand who our God really is. Go back through the psalm and list the aspects of God that show His power and ability to save and care for you.

When trouble comes, we all will have some type of response. This psalm is our guide: "God is our refuge and strength, a helper who is always found in times of trouble. Therefore we will not be afraid" (vv. 1–2).

As we meditate on who God is—a refuge, a river of the power of the Spirit of God, an immovable fortress—we can't help but begin to discover courage flowing through our veins. God is on our side. He is always available to help us!

The psalmist reflects on all the earth-shaking power of God, and then he offers us an invitation: "Come and see what the LORD has done, the desolations he has brought on the earth" (Ps. 46:8 NIV). Pastor Stuart Briscoe gives us an idea what this means: "If you want to see the bigger picture of desolation, go and have a look at that dank, empty tomb. He made the tomb desolate. He shattered it." That's the kind of desolation we can delight in! Again we're invited to "'come, and see what the Lord has done,' and if you're in trouble see your trouble in the light of what He has done."[3]

Finally, the psalmist calls us to respond by rejoicing in what the Lord promises. The second half of Psalm 46:10 says, "I will be exalted among the nations, I will be exalted in the earth!" (ESV).

Cease striving, and know that *our* God—an ever-present help in times of trouble, who makes wars cease and causes the earth to be removed and the mountains to fall into the sea—this fearsome and awesome God is with *you*. That truth, which we can *know*, will surely give us courage to face any circumstance, discouraging news, or trouble. For our God is *God*. That is cause for celebration. That is cause for us to offer Him our simple devotion.

Read the following passages and list what each says about God's strength and power.

Genesis 1:1–31

Genesis 18:9–14

Jeremiah 32:17

Matthew 19:26

_____

_____

_____

When you juxtapose your circumstances against who God is, what do you find happens to your outlook on your circumstances? In what ways does that help you to "be still"?

_____

_____

_____

_____

Look on page 106 at the different translations of the instruction in Psalm 46:10 to "be still." Which of those translations most resonates with you? Why?

_____

_____

_____

_____

What does this verse mean for how you might courageously live differently today?

_____

_____

_____

Reflect on this prayer and make it your own today:

God, I am overwhelmed and in awe of who You are. And You love me! And You have promised to help and rescue me when trouble comes my way. I truly have no reason to fear. Thank You! I praise You and rejoice in all You are and all You do. Amen.

being enough

"I know the plans I have for you"—this is the LORD's declaration—"plans for your well-being, not for disaster, to give you a future and a hope."

Jeremiah 29:11

Somewhere I hopped on the comparison train that circles the lie that at age forty I should have arrived at a certain level of success . . . in my career, in my personal relationships, in my health.

Needless to say, I am nowhere near where I thought I'd be in pretty much any area of my life. I thought I'd be full-on in a career. I thought I'd be married with children. I thought I'd have lost more weight. I thought. I thought. I compared. I compared.

The enemy wants nothing more than to distract us with idealized notions of our lives and what the world views as success. I have fallen victim to those distractions far too many times.

The Lord has so kindly and patiently showed me that not one of us is on a linear path. Rarely do we go directly from A to Z. Stories throughout the Bible remind us of this. Every one of those stories goes through countless highs and lows, numerous twists and turns. Each presumed setback was simply another opportunity to trust in the Lord and to put His glory on display.

So I'm not where I thought I'd be. That's not a totally bad thing. Yes, I do have a number of dreams that are not yet fulfilled. God has said that He isn't finished with me yet, and I believe Him. His Word will not return void. It will go forth and accomplish all it is meant to.

In other areas, I thank God I am not where I imagined I'd be. His plans are so much better than mine.

His thoughts are higher.

His ways are holy.

His timing is perfect.

He always has our good in mind because that's what a good Father does.

—KARINA ALLEN

Are you where you thought you'd be in your life? In what areas are you not in the place you dreamed of—career, marriage, family, location? How do you feel about the disparity between the life you imagined and the life you're living?

When our dreams for our lives don't come true and our hopes aren't met, many of us end up reeling from confusion and feeling "less than"—less than valuable, less than enough, less than important, less than significant. But that's not how God sees us.

In fact, God offers us a totally different view of significance. We can see it in Jeremiah 29:11, a popular verse that many of us like to quote when we think about our future. But before we consider that verse, we need to look at some of the background.

The Judahites had been carried off to exile in Babylon after Jerusalem fell to Nebuchadnezzar's army. The Lord's prophet Jeremiah writes to these captives to give them direction and encouragement (Jer. 29:1–3). This is what his letter to them says:

> This is what the LORD of Armies, the God of Israel, says to all the exiles I deported from Jerusalem to Babylon: "Build houses and live in them. Plant gardens and eat their produce. Find wives for yourselves, and have sons and daughters. Find wives for your sons and give your daughters to men in marriage so that they may bear sons and daughters. Multiply there; do not decrease. Pursue the well-being of the city I have deported you to. Pray to the LORD on its behalf, for when it thrives, you will thrive." (vv. 4-7)

In other words, the Lord, through Jeremiah, tells the exiles to make the most of their time in this place that isn't their home.

Read Jeremiah 29:7. What does the Lord command His people to do?

_____

_____

_____

_____

What is the Lord's promise if the Israelites do what He tells them?

_____

_____

_____

_____

It's difficult to wrap our heads around, isn't it? The Lord wants His people to pray for and work toward making their enemy's territory thrive—"for when it thrives, you will thrive." What an unusual directive regarding a place they had been taken to as captives!

The Israelites probably thought, *Wait, what? You want me to help my enemy succeed? That's the plan? That's my significance? Live my life—and as I'm living it, pray for them and do all I can to help my oppressors thrive?*

Would you be tempted to think that way if you were stuck in a place you had no say over? A place run by "an enemy"?

Perhaps you live in a town run by a differing political party. Or maybe you live in your in-laws' basement! Have you ever considered praying for and working toward their benefit? What might that look like?

Let's consider that we *are* actually living in a place that isn't our home. Hebrews 13:14 tells us that "this world is not our permanent home; we are looking forward to a home yet to come" (NLT). As Christ followers, we are exiles—foreigners, temporary residents, outsiders. We do not belong. This world is not our home; we live in enemy territory. And God is telling us that the most significant role we can play is to pray for our world and work toward making it thrive.

Have you ever thought of yourself as an exile? How does that change your perspective on your life?

_____

_____

_____

_____

In what ways do you think we thrive when the place we live in thrives?

_____

_____

_____

_____

Having dreams of being the next greatest doctor/lawyer/inventor/poet/president/you-fill-in-the-blank isn't wrong. Desiring marriage and a busload of children isn't wrong. Those are all wonderful and good goals to pursue. But none of those things make us significant; none of those things make us more or less valuable or valued by God. God may—and does—use those roles for His glory. But regardless of whether we achieve our dreams, God has an incredibly significant job for us—and it's simple and focused: pray for the world around us and work to make it thrive. That's it.

> **God has an incredibly significant job for us— and it's simple and focused: pray for the world around us and work to make it thrive.**

Whether you are in a leadership role or work at a minimum-wage, seemingly dead-end job. Whether you possess a position of far-reaching influence or your circle is small. Whether you are single, married, or single-again; a parent, an empty-nester, or without children; young, middle-aged, or retired—you have a great calling! Right where you are, right where *God has placed you.* You have been called to live as an exile in a world that isn't your home.

Let's continue in Jeremiah 29.

Read Jeremiah 29:10–14. How long did the Lord say His people would remain in captivity? And then what would happen (see v. 10)?

That's a long time to remain in captivity, isn't it? Yet think about our average life-span. Seventy years is an entire life. In other words, we live our entire life as exiles! This earth is not our home. Yet God promised that He would restore us to our rightful place—our true home—heaven. After God confirms this to the Israelites, He then offers a beautiful promise.

Read verse 11. How does that reflect and connect with the previous verses?

God's message to the exiles is clear: seek the well-being of the land you're living in, and He will restore you to your rightful home. Because God never changes, we can apply this idea to our own lives as outsiders!

Reread verses 11–14 in light of our exile status. In what ways does it change how you think about your significance and purpose?

Read John 17:15–18. What does Jesus pray for? How does this connect with us as exiles?

Look up Ephesians 2:10 and write it here.

What does this verse mean for how you might courageously live differently today?

Reflect on this prayer and make it your own today:

Father, I admit I forget that this world is not my home. Too often I try to find my significance in my roles or achievements—or I wallow in disappointment when life doesn't turn out the way I hoped. But You give me a hope and a future. You call me to something simpler. May I be faithful in praying for my world and in working toward making it thrive. Amen.

He said to me, "My grace is sufficient for you, for my power is perfected in weakness." Therefore, I will most gladly boast all the more about my weaknesses, so that Christ's power may reside in me.

2 Corinthians 12:9

For weeks my heart pounded every time I heard the tell-tale squeak of the mailbox. I'd rush to the front door, swing it wide open, and grab the stack of mail from the black box. I rifled through supermarket ads and bills, ever searching for a thick envelope holding my college acceptance letter. My heart was set on going to Stanford.

I was convinced that my impressive high school résumé—valedictorian, three-sport varsity athlete, four years of student government, glowing recommendations, and too many awards and activities and volunteer hours to count—would surely secure my elite-college dreams. I was an accolade junky destined for great things!

But that thick admissions packet never came. One day a flimsy rejection letter arrived in its place. My adolescent world crumbled around me.

I ended up going to a local state university. Their offer of a full academic scholarship would relieve the financial burden my family couldn't bear and save me from graduating with thousands of dollars of debt. Even so, I started into my collegiate journey stripped of my identity and weighed down with shame. How had I failed? How had all my hard work not paid off?

What I know now that I didn't know at eighteen is that Stanford's rejection was actually God's invitation. God wasn't devastating me, He was saving me—from myself. On the outside, my high school years may not have looked like typical teenage rebellion. But my heart was often devious, defiant, and always self-reliant. I believed my worth was based solely on how I performed, how I could impress and earn the approval of others. My pursuit of self-elevation and self-preservation left no room for God.

As God peeled back the layers of my sin in a place where no one knew my name or "fame," He rebuilt my identity on the truth: I am a child of God. Beloved by my heavenly Father not for what I do but for who He says I am—chosen, delighted in, forgiven.

I could no longer boast about the great things I was achieving or use a prestigious degree to impress people. But I did learn to boast in my deepening relationship with my Savior. God was impressing on my heart a whole new kind of hope and courage—not based on my own enoughness but firmly, simply rooted in His love and redeeming grace.

—BECKY KEIFE

Think about a time when you tried to rely on your own sufficiency and it didn't work out. How did you react? Looking back, do you see that "failure" as God-ordained? Why or why not?

The apostle Paul was a man who had a lot of accomplishments to boast about. Before Paul became a follower of Christ and "an apostle to the Gentiles" (Rom. 11:13), he was known as Saul, and he possessed quite an impressive résumé among the Jewish people. He was born in Tarsus, the capital city of the Roman province of Cilicia, making him not only a Jew but a Roman citizen—someone who carried a lot of influence. He was a strict Pharisee who was educated at the feet of Gamaliel, a well-known and respected teacher of the law and a leader of the Sanhedrin (the Jewish Supreme Court).[1] He was an authority within Jewish leadership circles and was present at and consented to the persecution of Christians—including the stoning death of Christianity's first martyr, Stephen (Acts 7:55–8:3; Acts 22:4).

Paul was proud of his accomplishments and took his authority seriously. He was from the right place, studied under the right person, held the right leadership role, hung out with the right people. Then he met Jesus.

Think about your own life. Do you perhaps take too much pride in being from the "right" place, school, business, or family? Why do you think that might be so important to you? If not, do you esteem others whose résumés appear more prestigious than yours?

Read Acts 9:1–22. Where was Saul traveling and for what purpose? What happened to him?

Think about how you first met Jesus and became a follower. What are some of the ways you remember encountering Him?

_____

_____

_____

_____

It's interesting to note that as Saul, renamed Paul, grew in his new-found faith and his understanding of Jesus, he had even more reasons to be esteemed: he was a leader of the church, an apostle, a church planter, a teacher, a healer, an academic, and on and on. Yet Paul no longer yearned for accolades or tried to impress others. He craved the simplicity of only one thing: to know Christ (1 Cor. 2:2).

What does Paul say we should boast about? See 1 Corinthians 1:31. What do you think he means?

_____

_____

_____

_____

Jesus's death on the cross for our sins and how that made a way for us to live as children of God is what kept Paul's focus. We see this as he responded to the boastful false teachers who wormed themselves into the Galatian church.

> As for me, may I never boast about anything except the cross of our LORD Jesus Christ. Because of that cross, my interest in this world has been crucified, and the world's interest in me has

> also died. It doesn't matter whether we have been circumcised or not. What counts is whether we have been transformed into a new creation. (Gal. 6:14–15 NLT)

That's really what our enoughness comes down to: that we have been transformed into a new creation. We are offered that transformation through Christ's act on the cross. It's that transformation that leads us to give our simple devotion to Jesus. But we've got to keep clinging to the truth of God's Word and of who we are in Christ Jesus. Paul understood this. And he wants us to understand it as well.

Our enoughness isn't about who we are, it's about who we are *in Jesus. He* is who we boast in. When we start to feel as though we need to be more, do more, have more in order to impress or fill our "enough" tank, we need to go back to who Jesus is. We need Jesus and nothing more. We stand firm when we stand at the foot of His cross. He has broken the power of sin over our lives (Rom. 6:1–11). He has given us the Holy Spirit as a Comforter and Counselor (John 14:16–17). He provides us with strength to live a holy and righteous life (Rom. 8:9). This indeed brings a simplicity to our focus; this indeed is something we can boast about!

> **Our enoughness isn't about who we are, it's about who we are *in Jesus*.**

Paul turned away from the need for accolades and clung to his new life in Christ. He writes about how we can turn our attention from boasting in our own sufficiency to boasting in our life in Christ. Read the following verses and list what Paul tells us to do.

> **Romans 12:1–2**
> **Ephesians 4:17–24**

Write 2 Corinthians 12:9 on a sticky note and place it where you can see it daily to remind you that boasting in your weakness glorifies God and strengthens you as you seek to live a simple life. What does this verse mean for how you might courageously live differently today?

_____

_____

_____

_____

Reflect on this prayer and make it your own today:

Thank You, Jesus, for Your sacrifice for me. Thank You that You are enough and that You make me a new creation—You transform me so that I don't have to try to be good or acceptable or valued on my own. Remind me that I can boast in You and Your work on the cross. Amen.

Whoever is faithful in very little is also faithful in much.

Luke 16:10

A neighbor's pine tree looms tall behind the fence in our backyard. Every day it generously sheds its needles onto our side of the fence, and every day we need to sweep them. It's a task you can't overachieve on one day so you can shirk it the next. It's an unavoidable daily chore.

This season seems to be full of unavoidable daily chores and mundane responsibilities. Laundry, packing school lunches, drop-offs and pick-ups, dinner prep, feeding the family, homework. The alarm rings at 6:30 the next morning, and it starts all over again. I never dreamt of being a stay-at-home working mom, and though the privilege of this season is not lost on me, there are days when I long for more than what my current life offers me. Motherhood shrank my world to the two little ones in front of me, but it was in the smallness that I began to understand that there is purpose in the mundane.

Mundane doesn't mean your life has no purpose outside of your little ones or loved ones. Small and quiet are not death sentences to your dreams and passions. Instead, they are simply a different framework in which God is doing His work. He is still being faithful to the work He's always been doing—to make Himself known to humankind and to reconcile us to Himself. This hidden season is fertile ground for Him to strip away what taints our character, to heal our wounds and brokenness, and most importantly, to tell us again and again that our purpose, our worth, our identity aren't found in life or ministry accomplishments. Our worth is found in our belovedness, our identity is grounded in Christ, and our purpose is to be like Him.

While the kids nap and quiet has been restored in the house, I slip my feet into my sandals and grab the broom. The pine needles need to be swept, and with each swish of the broom, I remind myself: this is my character being built, this is my identity being solidified, this is my purposeful, holy work.

—GRACE P. CHO

Though you know you're a new creation in Jesus and that makes you enough, are there still times when you struggle with the idea that you must do big things in order to validate your worth? Write about that here.

We've looked at who we are in and because of Jesus. Yet as we live as exiles in this temporary earthly home, the pressures of the world can begin to wear us down to the point that we start to give in to who the world *expects* us to be. And if we fail to live up to society's measure—if we fail to produce what's expected of us—then someone is sure to let us know.

That's the situation Hannah found herself in.

Read 1 Samuel 1:1–8. What big thing was Hannah unable to do? How did Peninnah make her feel about it?

Have you ever had someone taunt you over something you didn't have but they did? What was it? How did it feel? How did you respond to the person? How did you respond when you were alone with God?

In Hannah's time, polygamy was regularly practiced, and Hannah and Peninnah shared a husband, Elkanah. Though Peninnah had sons and daughters, the Bible tells us that Elkanah loved *Hannah* (v. 5). The Bible doesn't say that about Elkanah's feelings toward Peninnah. But Peninnah surely knew how Elkanah felt toward Hannah, because whenever Elkanah offered sacrifices for his family, he always gave portions of the sacrificial meat to Peninnah and her children, "but he gave a *double* portion to Hannah, for he loved her" (v. 5). And in the very next verses, we see Peninnah's response to Elkanah's act of kindness toward Hannah: "Her rival would taunt her severely just to provoke her, because the LORD had kept Hannah from conceiving. Year after year, when she went up to the LORD's house, her rival taunted her in this way" (vv. 6–7).

Every year Hannah received the same message loud and clear: *You aren't woman enough. You are nothing. Our husband may love you more—but I'm the one with the children. I'm the one who is really blessed.*

And it got to her! Her husband tried to comfort her: "Why won't you eat? Why are you troubled? Am I not better to you than ten sons?" (v. 8). But Hannah would not—could not—be comforted.

Maybe you painfully relate to Hannah's plight. Or perhaps the unrelenting issue in your life isn't about being a mother—maybe it's the unfulfilled desire to succeed in your career, to be a stay-at-home mom, to get married, or simply to be as smart or talented as someone else. Perhaps you're faced with anxiety every year at a holiday gathering, reunion, or conference, knowing someone is going to ask you if that area of your life finally meets their expectations.

Have you experienced the dread of going somewhere knowing you have to face a person who will undoubtedly send you the type of message that Peninnah sent Hannah? Write about it here, and share your pain as though you're offering it to God.

The world can be so cruel in the way it judges us. And when we begin to listen, the pain it evokes can feel devastating and cause us to question everything about who we are. Hannah was consumed by her anguish over Peninnah's constant jeering—as any of us in her situation probably would be. But *then* she made a choice.

Instead of continuing to wallow in her pain alone, Hannah turned her focus to the only One who could help and heal.

After she prayed, the Bible says she "went on her way; she ate and no longer looked despondent" (v. 18). Spending time with God in prayer can do that for us. He comforts us and gives us strength and peace as nothing else can. Has there been a time, after praying over something difficult, when you felt the Holy Spirit give you strength?

_____

_____

When others mock and ridicule us, or imply that we aren't as valuable as we should be, it's important for us to remember who God says we are and to cling to that singular and simple focus.

When the world says we aren't worthy, God says something *very* different. Listen closely to Paul's reminder from Romans 9:25–28 (MSG):

Remember who God says you are and cling to that singular and simple focus.

> Hosea put it well:
>
> I'll call nobodies and make them somebodies;
>   I'll call the unloved and make them beloved.
> In the place where they yelled out, "You're nobody!"
>   they're calling you "God's living children."
>
> Isaiah maintained this same emphasis:
>
> If each grain of sand on the seashore were numbered
>   and the sum labeled "chosen of God,"
> They'd be numbers still, not names;
>   salvation comes by personal selection.
> God doesn't count us; he calls us by name.

Reread this passage slowly and let each word sink in. Underline God's responses to how the world labels us. What does this say about how God feels about you?

_____

_____

_____

_____

Hannah's story gives us insight into God's heart. Peninnah mocked her, the high priest Eli rebuked her, but God *heard* her. He did not chastise her. He knew that "hope delayed makes the heart sick" (Prov. 13:12). He invites us—just as He invited Hannah—to bring our requests and pain to Him. And our pain will find a refuge in God.

Read Hannah's prayer in 1 Samuel 2:1–10. What strikes you about her prayer?

Spend some time asking the Lord to reveal places in your life where you've succumbed to feeling you must do big things or produce certain results in order to have value. Write what insights He brings to your mind.

Read Psalm 57:2 and write it here your own words. What does this verse mean for how you might courageously live differently today?

Reflect on this prayer and make it your own today:

Father, I need Your help to remind me that I don't need to produce anything to be valued. You have freed me from living under the world's expectations. I am Yours. Thank You for remembering and loving me. Amen.

Do not think of yourself more highly than you ought,
but rather think of yourself with sober judgment.

Romans 12:3 NIV

The retreat leader handed each of us paper and a pen with the direction to find a quiet spot and ask God to speak to us, then write what we heard the Holy Spirit say. I found a chair tucked in a corner and stared at the blank page, pen at the ready, feeling overwhelmed by the daunting task ahead of me.

What if I don't hear anything? I wondered. *What if everyone else comes back with amazing, prophetic words, and I still have a bunch of white space?*

I inhaled deeply and then prayed simply, "I'm here, Lord, listening."

Nothing.

I stared around, sighed quietly, and tried to keep my mind from drifting. I really hoped the Lord would say something like, *You're amazing. I just love you* so *much! You're doing great things for Me, working so hard. I'm grateful to have you as one of My followers.*

I knew it would be *highly* unlikely to hear those words, but a girl could hope. And if I were being honest, I kind of acted as if I were somehow doing God a favor by following Him. (That's painful to admit!) Even though during that particular season I was struggling both professionally and personally, I was forging ahead, trying to make it all work out and save my ego. Yet the harder I worked to take care of everything, the more I felt exhausted, insecure, and really grumpy. I felt like a failure—and I had gained more than fifty pounds in comfort eating that seemed to prove it!

I really wanted God to tell me I was okay.

I glanced at my watch. I had only five minutes left, and still my page was bare. I repositioned myself and put down the paper. That's when I heard it. The tiniest whisper.

You are not okay.

I blinked to keep the sudden tears from spilling onto my cheeks. *Great*, I thought, *even God is against me.*

My grace makes you whole, the still small voice said.

I sat stunned by the hard truth of what God revealed about me. I had been working so hard to show myself and everyone else that I am *somebody* that I had begun to believe the hype that says I am enough on my own.

Why do I do that? I wondered. *I know I am a sinner saved by grace. I know I am* not *okay on my own, but I keep acting as though I am!* It was like telling God, "Thank you for saving me, but now, really, God, I've got this." No wonder my life was in such disarray.

I sat for the remaining moments under the weight of conviction and grace, completely forgetting about that pad of paper. I had wanted my self-esteem to be lifted. I had wanted a rah-rah moment from God. Instead He revealed what I knew all along: that no matter what I try to do or how much I strive to be better, in my own self, *I* will never be okay. That's why I so desperately need a Savior.

That day I began a new journey—one in which every morning I awake and say, "In my own self, I am not okay. I am not enough. But Jesus in me is. And His grace makes me whole and righteous."

—GINGER KOLBABA

Have your actions or thoughts ever unintentionally communicated to God that you've got this handled? How has that worked out typically?

God loves us. A lot. Overwhelmingly. Deuteronomy 7:9 tells us that "he is the faithful God who keeps his covenant for a thousand generations and *lavishes* his unfailing love on those who love him and obey his commands" (NLT). If we're aren't careful, though, we may start to act as though He loves us *because* of something we've done. We forget that His transformative love doesn't come to us because we're so good and deserving or to make us happy. It comes to us because, in truth, we *aren't* good and deserving. And God is interested in making us holy more than happy. We need His loving grace to make us good enough.

The Old Testament prophet Isaiah learned about the "enough" of grace in a dramatic way.

Turn to Isaiah 6:1–5 and read about his vision.

Isaiah was a devout follower of God. He was a powerful prophet and was considered to be one of the holiest Israelites. He had a connection to the Lord that the other Israelites didn't have in which he received special revelations. God used him to communicate His message to the world and gave him special insight to see, spiritually speaking.

If anyone should have had the right to feel okay and enough, it definitely should have been Isaiah. He spoke *on God's behalf* to the people of Israel. God even blessed Isaiah by giving him a vision in which the Lord revealed Himself—"I *saw* the Lord" (v. 1). And yet when Isaiah saw the Lord, his first reaction was not to sing a happy praise song about how much God loves him. His first response was to recognize the reality of his own depravity.

Read Isaiah 6:5 again. What does Isaiah say?

Have you ever experienced God in such a way that it caused a similar response from you? Write about that here.

God allowed Isaiah to see the truth of who the prophet was apart from Him. But the Lord didn't leave Isaiah in his state of "not okay":

> Then one of the seraphim flew to me, and in his hand was a glowing coal that he had taken from the altar with tongs. He touched my mouth with it and said:
>
> Now that this has touched your lips,
> your iniquity is removed
> and your sin is atoned for. (6:6-7)

Isaiah confessed that everything we do—even our most righteous acts—are like filthy rags (Isa. 64:6). To be okay, we need God. And God, through His lovingkindness and mercy, provided a way to make Isaiah "good enough." He offers the same to us.

We are saved through grace, and we continue on the journey of becoming more and more like Jesus, a process called sanctification (see 1 Pet. 1:1–2). It is about living a holy and righteous life.

Read the following verses. Write in your own words what each means in light of being enough through God's grace.

2 Timothy 1:8–9

Titus 3:4–5

1 Peter 1:13–16

1 Peter 2:4–5

> The more time we spend with the Lord, the more we begin to grasp who we are apart from Him and how desperately we need His grace.

The more time we spend with the Lord, the more we begin to grasp who we are apart from Him and how desperately we need His grace. Because the truth is, no matter how much we strive or accomplish, we are not enough apart from God. A beautiful old hymn sums it up well: "I need thee, O I need thee; every hour I need thee. O bless me now, my Savior, I come to thee."[2]

Read Romans 12:3. How does Paul tell us to think of ourselves? What does this mean in light of striving to be good and enough on our own? What does this verse mean for how you might courageously live differently today?

Reflect on this prayer and make it your own today:

Father, forgive me for the times when I forget how much I desperately need You to make me holy. Help me to live in the light of Your grace—grasping a fuller meaning of who You are, what You've done for me, and what that means for my life. Amen.

One thing I do: Forgetting what is behind and reaching forward to what is ahead, I pursue as my goal the prize promised by God's heavenly call in Christ Jesus.

Philippians 3:13-14

After moving to a new city, it took my family almost two years to find a church home. We floated from one upbeat service to another, searching for a place that felt like the right kind of worship and preaching with a nurturing children's ministry. And if I'm honest, we spent a lot of Sundays in our pajamas—disheartened that our church wish-list wasn't matching our reality.

Finally, my husband and I decided we had to quit "church shopping" and choose to invest in a beautifully imperfect community. When we stopped making church about our preference and started making it a delight of our obedience, I experienced fresh joy and peace. My heart was hungry and finally open to worshiping God and receiving His Word in a new way. Instead of dreading the "where are we (or are we) going to church this week?" conversation, I looked forward to Sunday mornings!

Until a whisper changed everything.

We had been attending our new church regularly for several months and even had the pastor over for dinner. Everything was great. Then one Sunday in the middle of worship a sickening thought rose in my mind: *Look at the guy on stage. Doesn't he remind you of someone?*

How can you sing these songs to your God after what you've done?
Suddenly the worship leader bore resemblance in my mind to a person
I once dated—and all the sins of my youth flooded my heart like a tidal
wave of shame.

Never mind that I was happily married or that I hadn't seen this ex-
boyfriend in more than fifteen years or that I knew my sins had been
forgiven. I thought I was over this junk.

Yet Sunday after Sunday I couldn't get the images and poor choices
of my past out of my head. As everyone around me sang, I sank deeper
into my shame. Reasoning with myself that my teenager behavior
wasn't that bad compared to some, or turning my gaze to my husband
and adorable sons didn't help. The voice inside me only got louder. *You
shouldn't be here. Next time just stay home.*

Though I had known God for more than twenty years, I couldn't find
a way forward on my own. Finally, I confided in a friend and asked for
prayer. Together we asked God to remove the mental association I had
with the worship leader and grant me true and lasting freedom from
my past.

There's a difference between God's loving rebuke and the enemy's
sinister whispers. I had turned from my sin long ago, and God remembers it no more. It was the enemy alone who wanted to bind me back
up in a tangle of shame. But God is greater. Through the prayers of my
trustworthy friend and God's unending grace, I came to love Sundays
again.

I can now raise my hands in praise—and the only memories cours-
ing through my mind are of God's great faithfulness.

—BECKY KEIFE

Is there any area of sin that you thought you were over only to have past shame rear its ugly head again? How did God meet you in that place? Or where do you need to find freedom from sin today?

In and of ourselves, we can never be enough—but we were never supposed to be. As Isaiah 64:8 reminds us, "LORD, you are our Father; we are the clay, and you are our potter; we all are the work of your hands." He created us to need Him. We are not greater; He is.

Often, though, as we talk about not being enough on our own and needing God's grace to make up the difference, so to speak, the enemy of our souls can manipulate and twist that truth in order to deceive us. His crafty conniving goes something like this: *God doesn't really love you. His grace is for other people. How could it possibly be for you? Remember who you are—where you've been, what you've done. You'll never change. You really think He can forgive you for that?*

Satan pushes into our minds all the things from our past—shame, rejection, fear, addictions, adultery, depression, instability, guilt, mistakes. He may even bring up the irritated interaction you recently had with someone in which you said or did something that was all you and none of Jesus. And like judge and jury, the enemy knocks you down with a verdict of guilty, claiming you will never truly change. His constant goal is to remind you of every failure and negative label that has ever attached itself to you.

The Bible is clear that these are lies straight from the pit of hell.

Just as we need to understand who God is, what Jesus has done on our behalf, and who we are as we live in the enoughness of grace, we also need to understand what happens to our sin when we have been forgiven—and why it no longer holds us captive.

In Psalm 103, David makes it clear:

> For as high as the heavens are above the earth,
> so great is his faithful love
> toward those who fear him.
> As far as the east is from the west,
> so far has he removed
> our transgressions from us. (vv. 11–12)

How far has the Lord removed our transgressions from us (see v. 12)?

_____

_____

_____

_____

It's important to note that He not only takes away our sin but He does it out of His great love for us (v. 11). God's love is made evident by what He does. He is able to remove our transgressions beyond our ever being able to retrieve or remember them, because His love for us is in the same proportion—so high that we cannot fathom its end.

Some translations of verse 11 say it is God's mercy that is as high as the heavens (NKJV, for instance). The Revised Standard Version calls it His "steadfast love." Love, steadfast love, loving-kindness, mercy— why is the same Hebrew word translated so many different ways? The Hebrew word is _hesed_. One Hebrew scholar, Gesenius, thought it originally meant "keenness" or "ardent zeal."[3] As it appears in the Old Testament, then, it means an earnest goodwill, a love that is eager to help others. So God, in His love and mercy, doesn't simply throw away our sins—He eagerly does so. Does that sound like a God who holds grudges or rehearses our sins? No!

Verses 11 and 12 are closely tied together. Verse 11 gives the cause— God's mercy (loving-kindness, great love)—and verse 12 gives the result—God's forgiveness. One is impossible without the other. When the voice of the enemy whispers to our soul, *How many times do you think God will forgive you for that same sin?*, David answers, "As the heavens are high above the earth, so great is His *hesed* toward those who fear Him" (v. 11 NKJV).

The apostle Paul was a man of simplicity. He focused on glorifying Jesus in all he did. He could have let the sins of his past distract or deter him. But Paul understood that he needed God's grace to stay focused on the race ahead of him. We don't get far when we keep looking back.

Read Philippians 3:10–21. Summarize the key points in Paul's recipe for simple living.

In particular, let's look at Philippians 3:13–14. "One thing I do," Paul says. *"Forgetting what is behind* and reaching forward to what is ahead, I pursue as my goal the prize promised by God's heavenly call in Christ Jesus."

In order to reach forward, pursue the prize, and live with simple and pure devotion to Jesus, we must stop rehearsing the past—whether it happened a decade ago, last month, or yesterday. We confess, we repent, and we move forward by God's grace. Paul reminds us in Philippians 3:12 that we have not yet arrived. Hallelujah! But we pursue the things God has for us without carrying the weight of who we used to be.

> **In order to reach forward, pursue the prize, and live with simple and pure devotion to Jesus, we must stop rehearsing the past.**

Forgetting our past and not allowing it to control who we know we are in Jesus takes courage. It takes courage to confront the past and to say our behaviors and attitudes have no hold over us any longer. That God has thrown our sins as far as the east is from the west. That He remembers them no more. That we have been crucified with Christ and we no longer live but it is Christ who lives in us (Gal. 2:20).

Reread Philippians 3:12. What does this verse mean for how you might courageously live differently today?

Reflect on this prayer and make it your own today:

Father God, remind me of who I am and who I am reaching toward becoming more and more. Because of Your great mercy, I am no longer who I was. I am a new creation in You. Thank You that Your forgiveness has no end—no expiration date, no limit. Amen.

open-hands living

This is the way, walk in it.

Isaiah 30:21 NASB

I was standing over the kitchen sink, slowly and methodically rinsing strawberries, when I found myself thinking, *I really enjoy this*.

It wasn't life-changing. You wouldn't write home about slicing strawberries for a snack. The work was quiet, simple, easy. But the thought came and held on, and with it came a reminder that I learned the hard way: the spiritual practice of finding and choosing quiet causes something in our souls to twist up tight and then unwind with relief.

We're accustomed to doing one thing while thinking about or preparing for the next. Our thumbs scroll lit-up screens while we stand in line at the checkout counter. We are present but we are not. We slap on "busy" like it's a badge of honor, forgetting to breathe. Forgetting simply to be.

Several months ago, I stopped listening to music in the car. The to-do list continued to grow, my phone seemed to light up and ding at all hours, and quite frankly, something had to give.

There was simply too much noise, and my soul begged for quiet.

So I turned the dial off. Not down, *off*. I'm not sure where I was headed, but I distinctly remember the uncomfortable silence and an immediate pull to fill the emptiness.

As I sat in the quiet, the twisting inside slowly turned to relief. I didn't know how much my soul craved a moment of silence until the noise disappeared.

It began with a turned-off radio and eventually led to bowing out of opportunities, saying no more often, and standing over a sink, unhurried and happily rinsing strawberries. Over time, I found that choosing to slow down and rest is not a sign of weakness but of strength.

There's a time and place for noise, but our souls weren't created for hustling and rushing. We can't completely stop our lives to sit in silence for hours every day, but we can stop the glorification of busy. Somehow, someway, we can make space for silence, trusting that in the quiet we'll hear God speak.

Maybe it begins by simply turning off the radio.

—KAITLYN BOUCHILLON

Have you ever experienced that twisting inside that gradually turns to relief when you slow down and make space for quiet? How did it feel? Write about that experience here.

Living simply is big business. We have binders and plastic bins and cabinets to sort and organize and make our lives simpler. We can subscribe to magazines that devote their entire content to "real simple" living. And we can pursue simplicity with the same fervor and glorification that we chase everything else. In a way, the good thing we pursue can itself become an idol. Pursuing simplicity God's way is, well, much simpler. It doesn't require label makers or file folders. It requires one thing: focus.

Pursuing simplicity for simplicity's sake is not what God calls us to. He invites us to slow down and eliminate our internal and external clutter . . . in order to focus on Him. In the quiet of simplicity, we can better hear the voice of the Good Shepherd. And when we hear His voice, we can come when He calls, we can follow His ways. Focusing our minds on Jesus empowers us "to comprehend with all the saints what is the length and width, height and depth of God's love, and to know Christ's love that surpasses knowledge, so that you may be filled with all the fullness of God" (Eph. 3:18–19).

> **Pursuing simplicity for simplicity's sake is not what God calls us to. He invites us to slow down and eliminate our internal and external clutter . . . in order to focus on Him.**

Jesus practiced simplicity. He unplugged from the world and spent quiet time focusing on the Father. Perhaps we can't spend hours and hours in silence and solitude, but as Kaitlyn showed us in her story, we can gain simplicity through the small choices we make. Even in our normal tasks of life, like doing the dishes or vacuuming the rug, we can meet with and worship God. There is a sacredness to simplicity. Something mundane becomes a holy and pleasing offering. That's following Jesus.

Throughout the Gospels we read over and over Jesus's command to "follow Me." What comes to mind when you think of what it means to follow Jesus?

Lean in and listen to what the apostle John writes about the profound implications of following Jesus:

> We can be sure that we know him if we obey his commandments. If someone claims, "I know God," but doesn't obey God's commandments, that person is a liar and is not living in the truth. But those who obey God's word truly show how completely they love him. That is how we know we are living in him. Those who say they live in God should live their lives as Jesus did. (1 John 2:3–6 NLT)

This passage may not seem at first glance like it's about embracing simplicity, but John is clear—if we want to know God and live fully for Him, then we must obey His commands and live as Jesus did—or as the CSB translation says, "walk just as he walked." If Jesus commanded us to follow Him, then we best pay attention to the way He intentionally pursued simplicity in order to keep His wholehearted focus on the Father.

Have you ever thought that walking "just as he walked" includes practicing simple acts and silence? In what ways does this thought affect how you pursue simplicity?

Following Jesus boils down to this: we have to be quiet enough to hear Him. If our lives are busy and our focus becomes scattered, His voice gets drowned out. It's great to turn off the car radio or slice strawberries, but if our hearts aren't directed toward Jesus, these quiet moments become just another thing. Instead, Jesus says, *Follow Me . . .*

to the quiet. Follow Me . . . to the simple acts of just being in My presence. Follow Me . . . so you can hear My voice and go as I lead you.

The prophet Jeremiah gives us a sense of what following God and keeping that singular focus looks like. He writes, "You will seek me and find me when you search for me with all your heart" (Jer. 29:13).

In what ways does searching for God with all your heart help you follow Him?

_____

_____

_____

_____

What promises do the following verses offer as you follow Him in your pursuit of simple and pure devotion to God?

Psalm 91:14–15

Psalm 112:7

Jeremiah 24:7

_____

_____

_____

_____

As you pursue simplicity by focusing on Jesus and worshiping Him, how do you think your daily routine or mundane tasks might transform?

_____

_____

What holds you back from following Jesus with your whole life and heart?

Jesus says, "My sheep hear my voice, I know them, and they follow me" (John 10:27). Today as you prepare dinner or drive to work, during those moments when your mind goes in twenty different directions, allow yourself to breathe and focus on the most important thing—Jesus.

In what practical ways that work for your life can you slow down, be quiet, and listen to how Jesus tells you to follow Him?

Write out Matthew 11:29 in your own words as it applies to following Jesus.

What does this verse mean for how you might courageously live differently today?

Reflect on this prayer and make it your own today:

Jesus, I long to know Your voice intimately and follow You closely. That only really comes when I choose to slow down and focus on You in the simple ways. Sometimes this feels impossible. Help me to quiet the noise. Allow me to hear Your voice in those moments. Amen.

Abram believed the LORD, and he credited it to him as righteousness.

Genesis 15:6

It was three in the morning in the Lima airport in Peru when I received the email. I was somewhere between bleary-eyed and delirious. I clicked the email. A few words caught my eye.

We would like you to write a book . . .

I gasped. It was from a small publishing house in Nashville. I turned to the friend I was traveling with and waved my phone.

"A publishing house . . . wants me . . . a book!" I spurted out words that made no sense.

When my friend understandably didn't get what I was trying to say, I slowed my breathing enough to explain. It was my dream to be a published author, but I hadn't even written a book proposal. This publishing house had found my blog and liked what they'd read.

Over the next few months the publisher, editor, marketer, and I chatted. They were nothing if not kind. We conceptualized ideas, talked about titles, and looked over marketing plans. I was happily overwhelmed by the whole process—until one week when I started having nightmares.

I tossed and turned, and when I'd finally fall into a slumber, I awoke terrified. I lost all energy. I couldn't write. The thought of writing an entire book crippled me.

But I couldn't get these thoughts out of my head: *I am going to be published. This is what I've always wanted!*

I thought if I could get published, I would be seen as successful.

I thought if I could get published, I would finally have something worthwhile to tell people.

I thought if I could get published, I would be significant.

Yet, instead of peace and excitement, I was fraught with anxiety. After weeks of prayer and sleepless nights, I realized, *just because something is good doesn't mean it's right.*

Getting published was not inherently wrong, but my reasoning behind it was. Becoming a published author would not seal my significance. Writing a book to try and prove my worth to the world is not a good enough reason to write a book.

I took my shaky hands and typed an email. I clicked send and no longer had a book deal.

For a few minutes, I panicked, wondering if I had made the wrong choice. What if I'd just given away my one chance to be published?

Then I took a long, slow, deep breath, thanked God for His provision, and knew inexplicable peace.

—ALIZA LATTA

Have you ever experienced a time when what you wanted was within reach, but you realized you didn't have peace about it? Explain.

When we pursue the things we want or we believe God wants for us but then have an uneasy feeling about it, it's difficult to understand what's really going on. Sometimes God uses those things to see how focused we are on Him. Will we obey His leading? Our obedience shows that our heart is turned toward God. That we trust Him and believe His ways for us really are best. Having a simplicity of focus leads us to want to obey—and brings great reward.

God never forces us to obey Him. We get to choose. God's desire is for our obedience to be a response to receiving His love and loving Him back. Sometimes He calls us to do things we understand, things that make sense. When God calls us, for example, to simplify our lives by cleaning out our houses so we aren't overwhelmed with the piles, we can grasp how that is ultimately good for us. Sometimes, though, He calls us to do things we don't understand. Things that seem crazy. This is something Abraham discovered.

> **God's desire is for our obedience to be a response to receiving His love and loving Him back.**

In the Old Testament, the Hebrew word translated as "obey" means "to hear." Biblical hearing isn't a passive act but rather a responsive act of faith. To *hear* God's Word—what He calls us to do—is to obey (see Exod. 19:5; Jer. 7:23).[1] And to hear, we must remain attentive; we must remove anything that keeps us from that singular focus.

Abraham heard God. And in his hearing, he submitted and obeyed out of faith and trust. When God called Abraham to give up his homeland and everything he knew and held dear, Abraham said, "Yes, Lord," because he trusted God (see Gen. 12:1–9). As the years went by and he continued to follow God, God blessed him and his wife with a son. Isaac was no ordinary child, for God had promised that through this miracle child born from Sarah's barren womb, He would make Abraham a great nation (12:2).

So when Abraham heard God tell him to offer Isaac as a sacrifice to the Lord—in other words, God was directing Abraham to kill his promised child—he didn't argue. Wouldn't you expect that someone receiving that kind of news would become emotional and fret, run away, and disobey, or at the very least question God's goodness? But even though God's instructions made no sense, Abraham obeyed. Though he was potentially giving up his dream, he obeyed. Though he couldn't see the final outcome, he obeyed. Can you imagine that kind of faith? Abraham trusted God because he had seen His goodness and faithfulness to him over and over and over. God had promised good things for him. Did that make it easy for Abraham to walk forward in obedience with the intention of sacrificing his son? Absolutely not. Obedience can be painful. But Abraham's focus did not waver. He trusted that whatever happened, God would still be good.

Read Genesis 22:1–19. What happened when Abraham and Isaac got to the place where they would offer the sacrifice? What was the reward or blessing God gave Abraham (see vv. 15–18)?

_____

_____

_____

_____

Has God ever called you to give up something dear to you? What was it? Did you obey? Why or why not? What happened?

_____

_____

_____

Our obedience not only affects us, it stretches to others—generation after generation. Beyond what we can imagine. Hundreds of years after Abraham was willing to sacrifice Isaac, God rescued the Israelites from captivity and safely led them through the wilderness. Psalm 105:42–44 tells us that it was specifically because of Abraham's obedience, which God blessed:

> He remembered his holy promise
> to Abraham his servant.
> He brought his people out with rejoicing,
> his chosen ones with shouts of joy.
> He gave them the lands of the nations,
> and they inherited
> what other peoples had worked for.

What's even more wild to imagine is that because of Abraham's obedience, Jesus—the promised Messiah—ultimately came through his lineage (see Matt. 1:1–16). So much was riding on one person's simple focus on hearing God and responding in surrender. When God asks us to obey leadings that don't make sense to us, they may be part of a plan much bigger than ourselves.

How does Scripture describe what motivates us to obey God? See John 14:21, 23–24. How do you see this in your own life?

_____

_____

_____

_____

Reflect on this prayer and make it your own today:

Father, I long to hear You—the kind of hearing that leads to following. I love You and I know You love me. Remind me that even when obeying feels hard or scary or I don't understand how it will all turn out, I can trust You. You are so very trustworthy! Let my obedience be a reflection of Your great love. Amen.

Don't neglect to do what is good and to share, for God is pleased with such sacrifices.

Hebrews 13:16

W hat lovely earrings you have!" The woman sitting across our dining room table had been marveling at my mom's earrings all evening. Her eyes sparkled with curiosity at the ornately handcrafted jewelry from India, and as a young girl, I remember the way her compliment made me beam with pride for our culture and its beauty.

My mother smiled too, and then quickly replied, "Thank you! If you like them, you can have them." Within a split second, she took off the pearl-studded teardrops and handed them to our new friend.

It's an Indian custom to give what you have. Whether it's the rug in your living room or the bed on which you sleep, if you have something that someone else needs or even just simply enjoys, then you should give it to them, and with a joyful heart. As an Indian American woman, I was taught from an early age the value of generosity. It's a virtue that seamlessly interweaves with our cultural emphasis on honor and respect. Give what you have and give it joyfully.

This framework for generous living makes stories of the early church, like Acts 2:42–47 and 2 Corinthians 8, easy to understand. These men and women gathered daily and gave all they had to the poor. They held their resources—not just their money but even the possessions they loved—with open hands, so that they could give freely to anyone who needed them more.

I know many of us desire to live like this. However, sometimes the more expensive our belongings are, the harder they are to give away. We might cling tighter to a pair of earrings that cost sixty dollars or to a coat with a price tag in the hundreds. It is no mistake that the most generous people in the Bible were often the poorest. They had little, but they gave away much. This is the challenge for us today too. May we live simply and well within or even under our means so that we may be abundantly generous with all the Lord has given us.

—MICHELLE REYES

Have you ever been gifted something you saw and admired? How did that make you feel?

Do you find it easy or difficult to give things away? Explain.

In the Gospel of Mark, we see two instances of women who held loosely to their precious possessions in order to honor the Lord. In Mark 12:41–44, a poor widow's gift is small, nearly nothing. In Mark 14:3–9, the woman's gift is quite costly. Though Jesus praises both women, it isn't the gifts themselves that bring praise as much as their reasons for giving.

Let's look at each story.

In the first story, Jesus was teaching in the temple courts and sitting across from where people dropped their financial offerings into the temple treasury. Many rich people arrived and placed large contributions into the treasury. Their gifts would have been obvious to everyone.

"Then a poor widow came and dropped in two tiny coins worth very little" (Mark 12:42). A poor widow during that time would have been destitute. She would have had little opportunity to earn a living, and if she had no family, she had little hope for what one theologian calls "respectable survival."[2] Her two coins together amounted to about one-quarter of one cent.

When Jesus saw this woman and her gift, He turned His disciples' attention toward her. "Truly I tell you, this poor widow has put more into the treasury than all the others. For they all gave out of their surplus, but she out of her poverty has put in everything she had—all she had to live on" (12:43–44).

Contrast the widow's gift with the conduct of hypocrites as described in Matthew 6:2.

Think about your own giving to others and to God's work. How would Jesus classify it—out of your surplus or out of your sacrifice?

The second story takes place not long after the first. You'll be familiar with it from earlier in our study, but it bears mentioning again. Mere days before His crucifixion, Jesus was in Bethany relaxing among His followers, and "a woman came with an alabaster jar of very expensive perfume of pure nard. She broke the jar and poured it on his head" (Mark 14:3).

When some of the guests saw what she was doing, they began "expressing indignation to one another: 'Why has this perfume been wasted? For this perfume might have been sold for more than three hundred denarii and given to the poor.' And they began to scold her" (14:4–5). One denarius equaled one day's wage, so three hundred was almost an entire year's worth of income that this woman poured over Jesus. That's a lot of money! And that definitely could have helped a lot of poor people.

Jesus also could have scolded her for such waste. And yet He didn't. "Leave her alone," He told them. "Why are you bothering her? She has done a noble thing for me. You always have the poor with you, and you can do what is good for them whenever you want, but you do not always have me. She has done what she could; she has anointed my body in advance for burial" (14:6–8).

This woman offered an extravagant, extraordinary gift. So different from the widow's two meager coins. In what way, though, would you say their gifts were the same?

How does living out courageous simplicity allow us to give with an open-handed attitude?

In Acts 2:42–45, we read more about giving in the way the early Christians lived out their pure and simple devotion to God: "They devoted themselves to the apostles' teaching, to the fellowship, to the breaking of bread, and to prayer. Everyone was filled with awe, and many wonders and signs were being performed through the apostles. Now all the believers were together and held all things in common. They sold their possessions and property and distributed the proceeds to all, as any had need."

Acts 2:46 goes on to say that the believers continued "daily with one accord in the temple, and breaking bread from house to house, they ate their food with gladness and *simplicity* of heart" (NKJV).

Those who follow the ways of the world don't understand this kind of giving. They trust in money and material things. They stockpile and hoard. They may give out of their surplus, but they certainly wouldn't give everything, they wouldn't sacrifice till it hurts. And yet we give out of gratitude for all that God has done for us and for everything He has given us. And He owns it all anyway. We simply steward or manage it to the best of our ability.

> **We give out of gratitude for all that God has done for us and for everything He has given us. And He owns it all anyway.**

In what ways do you struggle with seeing giving the way the world does?

What stirs in your heart when you think about the idea that everything you possess is actually God's and you just get to steward it? In what ways does that change how you think about giving sacrificially to others?

According to the following verses, what happens to a generous person?

Proverbs 11:24–25

Proverbs 22:9

2 Corinthians 9:6–7

1 Timothy 6:17–19

Reflect on Hebrews 13:16: "Don't neglect to do what is good and to share, for God is pleased with such sacrifices." What does this verse mean for how you might courageously live differently today?

Reflect on this prayer and make it your own today:

Lord, all that I have and all that I am belong to You. Thank You for the ways You've provided for me. Grow my willingness to give to others and to You. Grow in me courageous simplicity so I can be courageously generous as an act of worship to You. Amen.

Those who know your name trust in you
because you have not abandoned
those who seek you, LORD.

Psalm 9:10

I was at a dead-end job. I was young and inexperienced, but educated and passionate. I wasn't respected, and having to take the owner's dog out to poop proved that. Yes, I was learning humility by the bucketloads while using a college degree and lots of hopes and dreams of future success to answer the phone, get coffee, and take the dog out to do its business.

Needless to say, I had plenty of time on my hands to think about my future. I was an aspiring young adult with grand plans for both my professional and personal life.

I was growing in my faith and praying about things I never had before, like my desire for a better job and to be married someday. I was reading business and relationship books while keeping my eyes open for Mr. Right. I had heard someone say that you should write a list of all the qualities you desired in a husband and pray over that list every day for the Lord to provide your Prince Charming. I was doing all the things I thought would lead to the life I wanted—the life God had planned for me.

One particular day I was extremely frustrated. I was over the job. Over the list. Over the way dating and relationships worked. I was finished with guys who wanted to hang out without any commitment, even as other people just assumed we were dating. I was fed up.

In that frustration, the Holy Spirit prompted me to turn to God. He nudged me to rip up my list, throw it in the trash, and keep my eyes on Jesus instead of on the horizon for a future job and my future man. I was open to whatever God had for me and to His best in all parts of my life.

A few weeks later, I started dating the man who would become my husband, and I received a job offer that came to me without requiring me to apply. God's dreams for me were much better than I could have planned or imagined. I'm glad I ripped up my own ideas to make myself open to what God had planned for me all along.

—STEPHANIE BRYANT

Think about a time in your life—maybe it's right now—when the thing you longed for felt out of reach. Did it occur to you to bring your desires and frustrations to God? Why or why not?

Have you ever felt the Holy Spirit nudging you to give up a list of wants and instead focus on what He wants for you? Describe what that was like and the courage it took to follow through.

Most of us have been in that place—working an unfulfilling job, wondering where Mr. Right is, asking ourselves, *Is this all there is?* You might still be in this place! Often our lives don't go quite the way we've planned or on the timetable we'd prefer.

The truth is that it happens all throughout life—not just when we're starting out in adulthood. We can be middle-aged and still wonder what we want to do "when we grow up." We can finally get married only to end up divorced and single again. We can finally become a mother and have children who grow up to worry us to no end with their rebellion and unwise choices. We can have the dream job and get laid off. And on and on. We can make our lists and become frustrated because we aren't checking off the items we've placed there.

As women of simplicity, at some point the Holy Spirit will nudge us with a prompt to realign our focus away from our wishes and to-do lists and back to the Lord. It takes courage to depend on God alone to meet our needs and trust that He has our best in mind. Right? But when we surrender ourselves and our lists to God, we allow Him to use our mundane days and lackluster seasons to shape our future as He wants.

> **Fear and worry fall away when we remember Whose hands we're in.**

That means that each day, each moment, we can choose to be fully present. This is essential to embracing simplicity. We direct our lists and our lives, our energies and our attention to where God leads us. Fear and worry fall away when we remember Whose hands we're in. As David writes in Psalm 16:5, "You, Lord, are all I have, and you give me all I need; my future is in your hands" (GNT). Later in Psalm 31:14–15 he writes, "I trust in you, Lord; I say, 'You are my God.' The course of my life is in your power."

Write out Psalm 16:5 and make it your prayer. How does it feel to own
those words? Is that deep level of trust in God and the future He has for
you congruent with what you actually believe? Why or why not?

Today we return to the Sermon on the Mount to examine what keeps
us from focusing on the Giver, and how Jesus realigns that focus out of
care for us.

In Matthew 6, Jesus teaches His disciples how to give (vv. 1–4), how
to pray (vv. 5–15), and how to fast (vv. 16–18). He then moves into how
we are to respond to our possessions, saying that we should hold them
with open hands while reaching for the treasures of heaven (vv. 19–21).

And then Jesus does what Jesus does best—He addresses the very
things He knows will hold us back from following Him fully.

Read Matthew 6:25–34. Listen to the words of Jesus and hear Him
speaking them directly to you. As He speaks, what concerns come to
your mind?

Essentially, Jesus is answering the "Yes, but . . ." argument He knows so many of us go to. "Yes, Lord, I know this is how You want me to live, but what if . . . ?"

The implied message we offer is, *What if I trust You with all these things, with living this way, and hold loosely to my life and my wants—what if I totally abandon myself to You and it doesn't work out?* Our minds go to those worst-case scenarios, don't they? What we're really asking is, *God, are You truly trustworthy?* Giving Him our list is scary, it's risky! And what if *this time* God doesn't prove faithful? *What if I give and pray and fast and pursue treasures in heaven, and You don't live up to Your end?*

Jesus responds by addressing our fears head-on: "Don't worry about your life" (6:25).

What is one item on your list of dreams that you ache over but fear God has forgotten about? Write what you hear Him telling you about it.

God's heart for you is so clear. He wants for You to know Him fully—and to trust Him completely. Giving up that control takes courage. What character traits does someone possess who has given herself fully to God (see Luke 9:23–25; 2 Cor. 5:14–15)?

"Those who know your name trust in you because you have not abandoned those who seek you, Lord" (Ps. 9:10). What does this verse mean for how you might courageously live differently today?

Reflect on this prayer and make it your own today:

Father, forgive me for the times I've focused more on the gifts You might give me than on You, the Giver. Send reminders of Your faithfulness to soothe my soul in the places it's frayed with worry. Grant me the courage I need to trust You completely. Amen.

Everything that was a gain to me, I have considered to
be a loss because of Christ.

Philippians 3:7

I am a recovering collector, especially of Christmas items. Ornaments, recipes, books, CDs, movies, and decorations. If it could be collected, it was likely that I had it. I worked at a Hallmark store for years, which made it easy for my collections to grow and grow.

One year, my husband and I unloaded our bins of Christmas decorations into our new-to-us townhome. We'd been married a couple years, this was the first home we owned, and we were excited to decorate it for the holidays! My collections were at their peak, and I was thrilled to finally have a space in which to display them all.

After unpacking the bins of decor, we stepped back to admire our handiwork and realized it looked like Christmas had thrown up in our little house. There was no space between one decorated area and another—every surface was covered with holiday stuff, and it was *just . . . too . . . much.*

We needed open space for the beautiful decorations to be properly highlighted and enjoyed.

We went through the house and took down every single thing that we didn't absolutely love. That helped. And each year since, if an item is not meaningful to us and/or if we don't truly love it, it goes into an empty bin. Then at the end of the season, we donate whatever is in that bin. Truth be told, this is something we practice year-round, not just at Christmas and with holiday items.

Since that first house, our number of decor bins has decreased significantly, and so have my collections. We're now left with only the items we cherish. It's a more visually peaceful space to enter, with less stuff crowding it and much more room to breathe.

Much as I love my collections, having less of them actually makes each item more significant and special. The simplicity of fewer *things* allows the peace of God to shine through, rather than having to fight for space among so much stuff.

—ANNA RENDELL

Have you ever looked around your home and felt as though the amount of stuff was crowding out the peace? What do you typically do when your stuff begins to feel like too much?

Several years ago, Marie Kondo, an organizing expert, wrote a book that took North America by storm.[3] In it she encouraged her readers to release and get rid of items that didn't bring them joy. The idea was that by holding on to too many things, we lose the ability to simply relish what we do possess. One piece of practical advice she offered was to start with our closets. We should remove everything and put it into one big pile. Within three minutes, we must go through the pile and decide with each item, "Does this bring me joy?" If not, it goes out the door.[4] Her motto? "Tidy your space, transform your life."[5]

The truth is, holding on to too many things usually says much more about our spiritual lives than about our physical surroundings. This was a point Jesus made when a wealthy young man came to Him and asked to be one of His disciples.

> **Holding on to too many things usually says much more about our spiritual lives than about our physical surroundings.**

Turn to Mark 10:17–27 and read the story.

Before your palms get too sweaty, Jesus is probably not asking you to sell everything you own! More than an all-call for selling all our possessions, Jesus is addressing a heart issue: He is asking the man, "Which do you love more—Me or your things?"

The beautiful part of this story is that Jesus doesn't lecture the man or rebuke him. Verse 21 tells us that Jesus loved him. That's the key to understanding this passage. Jesus never asks us to give up anything through guilt. He asks us to hold loosely to the things of this world and focus on Him because He loves us and knows what will bring us true joy. He's inviting us to put our energy into something greater than objects that will eventually break or fade away. Even the most sentimental items we love will someday be lost when we leave this world. Why cling to those when we can cling to the eternal—to the things of God?

Read Luke 12:15–21. What does the man in this story do with his goods? What is his reasoning? What happens to him?

This story is a harsh one to read, because God forces us to face our spiritual motives. "You fool!" God tells the man in verse 20. "This very night your life is demanded of you. And the things you have prepared—whose will they be?" The man who hoards stuff in case he needs it someday doesn't even survive to the next day. We find Jesus isn't just telling a story; He means it when He then says, "That's how it is with the one who stores up treasure for himself and is not rich toward God" (v. 21). *Gulp.*

How familiar this scenario is to many of us. We own so many things that, like the man in Jesus's story, we wonder what to do with all of the excess because we don't have enough storage. The man didn't decide to sell or donate his surplus so that others could benefit; he kept it for himself so he didn't have to worry about the future. It's interesting that we're back to that worry or fear problem again, isn't it?

That same chapter (Luke 12:22–24) shows us the simplicity that God wants us to live in. Jesus reminds us that the birds don't have storerooms or barns, and yet God provides everything they need.

The apostle Paul writes, "Everything that was a gain to me, I have considered to be a loss because of Christ" (Phil. 3:7). What does this mean to you as it relates to holding our possessions with open hands? Rewrite this verse in your own words.

In what ways does losing have its benefits? Physically? Emotionally? Relationally? Spiritually? Ecclesiastes 3:6 says there is "a time to seek,

and a time to lose; a time to keep, and a time to cast away" (ESV). What might God be calling you to cast away?

_____

_____

_____

_____

Ponder and pray about the areas in which you feel pressured to acquire more. List some of them here. How does this pressure affect your lifestyle? What would God say about it? Ask the Holy Spirit to give you discernment in this area. Write your observations.

_____

_____

_____

_____

Read Philippians 4:11–12 in *The Message* (you can read it through Biblegateway.com or a Bible app). Let the words sink in. Can you say this about your own life? Why or why not? What does this passage mean for how you might courageously live differently today?

_____

_____

_____

_____

Reflect on this prayer and make it your own today:

Father, I hold onto the things I own because I think they will bring me joy. But really my stuff showcases how I sometimes desire stuff more than You. Forgive me. Show me how I can declutter my life and heart. I want to be free to focus on You. Amen.

embracing the peace that comes

Just as you have received Christ Jesus as LORD,
continue to live in him, being rooted and built up in him
and established in the faith, just as you were taught,
and overflowing with gratitude.

Colossians 2:6–7

My hands, clasped tight, jostled up and down with the rhythm of the train. On this first of many commutes downtown, I sat in the first car and tried to pray as building after building passed by. Today marked the first day of a new job, and I had all the typical emotions connected with that.

I was excited and nervous, giddy and terrified. A million thoughts raced through my mind. I wanted to do well today, to do great things and make a mark. I wanted to be confident, to make it look as though I belonged. As I was praying for these things, something made me pause. Something didn't feel right. As the doors of the train opened and closed yet again, I wondered about my prayer. What was I really praying for and why?

In the midst of my desire to impress and succeed, I had forgotten to express simple gratitude to God for this new job. I had been so focused on myself that I had lost sight of God's hand and sovereignty over it all. I wouldn't even have this job without His divine orchestration.

Immediately my prayer changed course. I began praying a simple list of thank-yous. I thanked God for giving me this job. I thanked Him for opening this door, for bringing me to this place, for making this dream possible.

Then I began looking around. My eyes gazed out the window and watched the rising sun. I thanked God for this new day, for His mercies and faithfulness in my life. The more things I found to be grateful for, the more I was able to breathe deeply and relax my body and mind. In fact, by the time I stepped off the train, I felt full of joy and peace.

It's amazing how powerful humble gratitude can be. Remembering what God has done is a simple way not only to calm our nerves but more importantly to reorient our focus and give thanks in any circumstance.

—MICHELLE REYES

Have you ever been anxious about something and chose to focus on gratitude to God instead of the object or circumstance bringing anxiety? How did that affect you? Or if you're tangled with worry or anxiety today, write about that here.

One of the most special aspects of simplicity is what it brings out in us. As we slow down and take in the joy and preciousness of life, we discover how much we truly have to be grateful for. God has blessed us beyond what we can possibly ever know or even imagine. Take a few moments and jot down some blessings that come to mind.

_____

_____

When we let the reality of God's constant presence and unfailing goodness become our greatest focus, guess what's going to follow? Joy, peace, and a desire to worship God with everything we've got.

Watch how this plays out in David's life through his words in Psalm 63. David had been in a wilderness, both literally and figuratively. While we don't know for certain what particular challenge David was facing when he wrote Psalm 63, we do see clearly what came out of his wilderness experience: gratitude and praise.

Let's read Psalm 63:1–8 (MSG) together:

> **When we let the reality of God's constant presence and unfailing goodness become our greatest focus, guess what's going to follow? Joy, peace, and a desire to worship God with everything we've got.**

God—you're my God!
  I can't get enough of you!
I've worked up such hunger and thirst for God,
  traveling across dry and weary deserts.
So here I am in the place of worship, eyes open,
  drinking in your strength and glory.
In your generous love I am really living at last!
  My lips brim praises like fountains.
I bless you every time I take a breath;
  My arms wave like banners of praise to you.
I eat my fill of prime rib and gravy;
  I smack my lips. It's time to shout praises!
If I'm sleepless at midnight,
  I spend the hours in grateful reflection.
Because you've always stood up for me,
  I'm free to run and play.
I hold on to you for dear life,
  and you hold me steady as a post.

In this psalm David reflects what is fundamentally true for all of us: an undeniable longing for God. He likens his need for God to the person dying of hunger and thirst in a desert (v. 1). When someone has that kind of hunger and thirst, their focus is on one thing and one thing only: having it satisfied and quenched.

Reflect on a time when you experienced a wilderness. How did God sustain you? Did it make you more or less hungry and thirsty for God? Explain.

Looking back, what about that experience fills your heart with gratitude?

God places that spiritual longing within us—knowing that only He can quench and satisfy it. Read the following verses. What does Jesus offer us? How does He describe Himself?

Matthew 5:6

John 4:14

John 6:35

Jesus is referring to the deep, abiding satisfaction that comes to those who receive and embrace Him as their Savior. He satisfies completely. And as we continue to abide in Him, He continues to feed us. As Jesus says in Matthew 4:4, "It takes more than bread to stay alive. It takes a steady stream of words from God's mouth" (MSG).

David found his ultimate satisfaction in God (Ps. 63:5) and expressed it using the idea of eating his fill "of prime rib and gravy; I smack my lips. It's time to shout praises!" That pleasure and contentment lead us back to gratitude.

No doubt at one time or another you have experienced an inner spiritual hunger that craves satisfaction. The remedy is not to drown it, drug it, suppress it, overschedule it, or crowd it out. Rather, God's remedy is clear:

> Is anyone thirsty?
>   Come and drink—
>   even if you have no money!
> Come, take your choice of wine or milk—
>   it's all free!
> Why spend your money on food that does not give you
>   strength?
>   Why pay for food that does you no good?
> Listen to me, and you will eat what is good.
>   You will enjoy the finest food. (Isa. 55:1-2 NLT)

Water, wine, and milk are figurative terms to indicate how the blessings God offers are designed to nourish the soul as well as to make it glad and cheerful. The prophet Isaiah is telling us that if we long for fellowship with God, it is ours for the taking! God is telling us to *gorge* ourselves on Him. He is our feast.

What comes to mind when you hear this invitation from Isaiah? What has it looked like or what could it look like in your life to feast on Jesus this way?

Write out Colossians 2:6–7 in your own words, as though you are writing it to encourage yourself.

What do these verses mean for how you might courageously live differently today?

Reflect on this prayer and make it your own today:

Lord, how can I even begin to thank You for all You've done for me? I hunger and thirst for more of You. Fill me, Father! May I seek to be nourished and satisfied by You alone. Amen.

Jabez called out to the God of Israel. . . . And God granted his request.

1 Chronicles 4:10

When my husband, Dan, was diagnosed with a serious illness, I couldn't find the "right" way to ask God to heal him. I struggled to pray big enough words—in strong and potent-sounding petitions worthy of God's great healing power. In my limited view, other people in the world had such serious problems—war, famine, poverty, natural disasters—that Dan's personal problem, while serious, didn't compare. What could I say that would match his need but be grand enough to honor God?

Then one day, during our morning prayer time, I heard my husband simply ask, "Dear Lord, please heal my disease."

It was such a plain but heartfelt plea that it reminded me to stop complicating every prayer request, because God perfectly hears our simple cries for help. As David simply asked, "Be gracious to me, Lord, for I am weak" (Ps. 6:2).

Evangelist Charles Spurgeon declared of David's simple request, "This is the right way to plead with God if we would prevail. Urge not your goodness or your greatness, but plead your sin and your littleness."[1]

Be simple and small in such prayer moments—because God is already great. Thus, our words don't have to be.

That's what David showed during a time of spiritual confusion and despair. "Turn, Lord! Rescue me," he writes in Psalm 6:4. His exact situation isn't explained in this psalm. His simple plea, however, shows a deep desire for God's help—exactly because his words *are* so ordinary. "I am weary from my groaning" (v. 6). This simple honesty, offered unto God, says it all.

No, this isn't a fancy prayer or an elaborate plea. But David's ordinary words show it can be enough simply to tell God, "*Help!*"

David rejoices, "The Lord has heard my plea for help; the Lord accepts my prayer" (v. 9).

Even a simple one? Yes, because my simple prayer shows this: I trust God with all.

—PATRICIA RAYBON

How often have you felt as though simple prayers aren't enough to get God's attention or to sway Him to act on your behalf? Why have you felt that way?

The Bible is filled with prayers and pray-ers. We can find pleas to the Lord for all kinds of troubles or desperate situations. But they all share one common trait: they are prayed from hearts of simple and pure devotion to God—and without fail, God hears and answers.

Let's turn our sights to a seemingly obscure man in the Bible—Jabez. We find his story in 1 Chronicles 4:9–10:

> Jabez was more honored than his brothers. His mother named him Jabez and said, "I gave birth to him in pain."

> Jabez called out to the God of Israel, "If only you would bless me, extend my border, let your hand be with me, and keep me from harm, so that I will not experience pain." And God granted his request.

First Chronicles 4 is a genealogical record of Jacob's son Judah. Verse after verse goes through his family tree, so that by the time we reach verse 9, our eyes might be tempted to skim over Jabez. But don't! The details accompanying Jabez's lineage show us an example of a courageous and faithful prayer in action.

Jabez's name means "he causes pain." In ancient Near Eastern culture, the meaning of names was significant. Jabez was concerned with the potentially prophetic nature of his name, so he prayed a very simple yet bold prayer requesting that he would not live a life of pain.

Though some may read Jabez's request as a request for prosperity, we lose the bigger meaning if we follow that line of thinking. Jabez was requesting provision, not prosperity. He submitted his desires and needs to God, believing God would set him on the right path according to His will.

Jabez prayed for God to be with him and to protect him from being a Jabez. In other words, as Matthew Henry says, he prayed that God "would keep him from evil, the evil of sin, the evil of trouble, all the evil designs of his enemies, that they might not hurt him, nor grieve him, nor make him a Jabez indeed, a man of sorrow."[2]

And God granted Jabez's request: He prospered him and gave him success in his work and relationships, and thus Jabez became "more honored than his brothers" (v. 9).

How does Jabez's prayer align with the way Jesus taught us to pray? See Matthew 6:5–15 (in particular vv. 7–8).

According to Romans 8:26, when we don't know what or how to pray, what comfort does Paul tell us we have?

_____

_____

_____

Jabez wasn't asking for something outside of God's will. He was offering a faithful submission to God's will in his life. He was simple in his request, just as God calls us to be.

As you go to God with your requests, heart surrendered to His will, how do the following verses encourage or guide you?

    1 Chronicles 16:11   Romans 12:2

    Psalm 145:18   Colossians 4:2

    Matthew 26:41   1 John 5:14

_____

_____

_____

_____

God calls us to lay down our wants and our "deserves" and seek His kingdom *first*. As Jabez understood, we must trust God's best for our lives, His knowledge of the bigger picture, and His desire to help us become more like Jesus. He uses everything to accomplish that will. Our prayers aren't simply to ask for things—they are an invitation to experience trust and intimacy with Jehovah-Jireh, our Provider.

Sometimes God calls us to be patient as we pray. Sometimes He tells us no—but we can be assured that the no is for a good reason. Sometimes our prayers are lessons in holding lightly to the things of this earth so that we can draw closer to the Father's heart in the process (see James 4:8). As we pray and intimately connect with God, we begin to see that everything we *really* want, need, or deserve are the things we already have—in Christ.

God calls us to lay down our wants and our "deserves" and seek His kingdom first.

One simple way to pray is by praying back the Scriptures to God. For God tells us through His prophet Isaiah, "My word that comes from my mouth will not return to me empty, but it will accomplish what I please and will prosper in what I send it to do" (55:11). Pastor John Piper uses the acronym IOUS from the Psalms as a guide to praying the Scriptures:

I: Incline my heart to your testimonies (Ps. 119:36)

O: Open my eyes to see wonderful things (Ps. 119:18)

U: Unite my heart to fear your name (Ps. 86:11)

S: Satisfy me in the morning with your steadfast love (Ps. 90:14)[3]

And on days when you're out of words or don't know what to say, all you truly need to do is to be still and pray, "Speak, Lord." Then listen to His voice.

Look again at 1 Chronicles 4:9–10. Write Jabez's prayer in your own words. How does this prayer change for you when you view it as a plea for seeking God's heart rather than a request for material prosperity?

What does the prayer of Jabez mean for how you might courageously live differently today?

Reflect on this prayer and make it your own today:

Father, thank You that nothing I pray for surprises You, because You know everything about me. Thank You that I don't have to pray using sophisticated or poetic language. Give me courage to pray with simple boldness. Thank You for always hearing me. Amen.

The peace of God, which surpasses all understanding,
will guard your hearts and minds in Christ Jesus.

Philippians 4:7

I n the chaos of after-school pickup, I saw a mom I knew, and in an attempt to briefly connect with her, I said, "It's *so* hot right now, isn't it?" I meant it to be a quick and light conversation to commiserate together as we waited for our kids, so I was caught off guard by her response and subsequent advice.

"It is, but not as bad as when my kids play soccer at five o'clock! Are your kids in soccer? You really should put them in something—the earlier the better."

She chided me with the tone of her voice and the look on her face. And though she meant well, the underlying message was that I wasn't doing something right as a mom. That my kids were lacking something because we weren't involved in after-school activities.

We're one of the few families I know who aren't busy with sports or dance or anything else, and it's a conscious decision my husband and I have made. But the culture around us says we should be providing as many opportunities as possible for our kids and that busyness is simply a side effect of the best life we could live.

But in hustling after the "best" life, I've seen no margin for people just to be or to experience peace as they rush from one thing to the next. That's not the kind of life I want for me or my family.

And yet, when my friend advised I should be doing more for my kids, I couldn't help but feel the pressure of her words squeeze my convictions into naïve notions. For several days, I weighed out the pros and cons, wondering how we could do more for the kids while maintaining the simple life we currently have.

In the end, I realized there's always a cost to the decisions we make, even when they're a no. Perhaps others might say my kids don't have enough because we don't *do* enough for them, but instead of the "best" life, we have a peaceful life, and that is what's best for us.

—GRACE P. CHO

Do you ever feel pressured by others to do more? How do you handle the temptation to strive for what others say is best?

A peaceful life. That's what we all long for, isn't it? As we've traveled through this study, hopefully a greater sense of peace has settled over you, the kind of peace that comes when life aligns with God's desires for you. You probably haven't arrived completely at a full life of simplicity—you still have moments when the old ways demand your attention. And yet, as Grace discovered, those ways no longer hold promise. You see those ways for what they are: vapid, empty, unfulfilling. Hopefully you are realizing more and more how much life's distractions have shaped you: the constant state of motion, the multitasking. Saying no to those ways and pursuing simplicity is becoming easier. Less guilt! Less tension and stress! Though responsibilities still require your attention—you still have work, family, friends, and community to care for—you are learning better to put your priorities in check. You don't allow those responsibilities to dictate the state of your mind and soul any longer.

You are practicing being solely present and in the moment. You know God is pleased with your choices when you choose the simpler way—He's pleased because you are looking solely to Him for your guidance and fulfillment. As the psalmist writes, "Taste and see that the LORD is good. How happy is the person who takes refuge in him!" (Ps. 34:8). And you have! Not only have you tasted, you are gorging yourself on God's goodness. You are focusing a simple and pure devotion on Him. Can you start to feel more joy and calm? Once you experience the life of simplicity, you'll never want to go back to the way things were when you were distracted and too busy and believing the lies that accused you of not being enough.

Read Proverbs 2:1–6. How might following this teaching help you prioritize your life to keep it simple?

Prayerfully consider how God wants you to best use your time and energy. Write below what you hear Him telling you.

Even when we make progress in simplifying our lives and we experience the daily joy of God's presence, the battle isn't over. The enemy doesn't like when we find rest and peace. He waits for us to be so comfortable that we become lax. That's the perfect time for him to strike out at us. When we let our guard down, we slowly make compromises to our peace and let little bits of the world's messages and glitz and glory seep into our lives. The apostle Peter warns us of this in 1 Peter 5:8, where he writes, "Be sober-minded, be alert. Your adversary the devil is prowling around like a roaring lion, looking for anyone he can devour." Paul also warns us, "Be careful that no one takes you captive through philosophy and empty deceit based on human tradition, based on the elements of the world, rather than Christ" (Col. 2:8).

Protecting your new commitment to living simply starts by coming with your whole self, quiet before the Lord each day. Asking Him to guide you through your schedule and your relationships, asking for a focus that allows you to be present in each interaction without allowing distractions to overtake your time or attention.

> **Protecting your new commitment to living simply starts by coming with your whole self, quiet before the Lord each day.**

If we want the best life now, then we need wisdom to know the difference between the world's best and God's best. So let's make Psalm 90:12 our prayer: "Teach us to number our days carefully so that we may develop wisdom in our hearts."

Look up Mark 12:28–31 and 1 Corinthians 10:31. When you think about pursuing a life of simplicity, how do these passages serve as a lens for discerning how to spend your time wisely?

The beauty of living in simplicity's peace and cherishing what truly matters is that you realize it's okay to say no to the expectations that lay and prey on you. The only expectations you need to consider are God's. And God's expectations are never too much for us because He promises to carry it all with us. "Take my yoke upon you," Jesus says. "Let me teach you, because I am humble and gentle at heart, and you will find rest for your souls. For my yoke is easy to bear, and the burden I give you is light" (Matt. 11:29–30 NLT).

Write out the following verses. How might they encourage you as you seek to stay present for the things that truly matter?

    Psalm 25:4–5

    Psalm 25:9

    Psalm 32:8

"Teach us to number our days carefully so that we may develop wisdom in our hearts" (Ps. 90:12). What does this verse mean for how you might courageously live differently today?

Reflect on this prayer and make it your own today:

Father, give me wisdom to stay alert and know how to respond to the world's message that I should do and be more. Show me how to deal with interruptions and distractions that come my way. Let me be fully present and focused on what You have for me today and every day. Amen.

Not that I have already reached the goal or am already
perfect, but I make every effort to take hold of it
because I also have been taken hold of by Christ Jesus.

Philippians 3:12

For years I saved candles. Stored in cabinets or displayed on shelves, they sat waiting for "the right day" or "the best time." Each unlit wick told the story: at some point along the way, I began to act as if candles were only meant for parties, celebrations, or magical moments.

So they sat gathering dust day after day, month after month.

It wasn't until I began to see there could be meaning in the mundane and glory in the common and beauty in the ordinary of right now that I reached for the lighter and watched wisps of smoke waft into the air.

It's a simple thing. Just like using the good china for a regular Tuesday evening meal, lighting a candle won't change the world. But it changes how I see the world. Maybe, in some small way, those are the same thing.

Maybe this right here is holy.

We have only this ordinary moment to live and love well. Maybe we'll receive another day, another year, a decade or two, but none of us truly know. We're part of the greatest story ever told, but we don't hold the pen.

Lighting a candle is not the answer to all our problems. It won't end world hunger, solve global warming, or eliminate human trafficking.

But when it seems like the world is going up in flames, maybe the small and simple act of lighting a candle on a regular day is one way to push back the darkness. It reminds us that we are still reaching, still lighting, still living.

The cabinets once filled with candles are almost empty now, but they tell a new story. As I reach for the lighter every evening, I practice paying attention, reminding myself that there's beauty in today. God is here, He is with us, and the story isn't over just yet.

This is the beautiful and ordinary right now.

—KAITLYN BOUCHILLON

Do you have items that you use only for special occasions? Have you ever considered using them for everyday moments? Why or why not?

_____

_____

_____

We are on a journey that's transforming us to be more like Jesus. As Isaiah 64:8 says, "Lord, you are our Father; we are the clay, and you are our potter." We don't one day wake up and find that we have arrived at perfection or simplicity. It's a process—and the molding and shaping of our lives so often takes place in the middle of the simple and mundane. God leads us more into holiness through the ordinary than through the extraordinary. Those are the moments when He is silently at work, asking us to be patient, telling us that the story isn't over, that the waiting is part of the experience of following God and becoming Christlike. That is the hope we profess and cling to, that we are becoming and will eventually become everything we were created to be—"since he who promised is faithful" (Heb. 10:23). That means we don't have to try to force the simple life; we accept it as a sacred rhythm for our daily lives.

As we become more like Christ, we learn to see and appreciate the holy in all of living—in navigating our trials, certainly, but also in hearing the laughter of our children, in lighting candles or using our good china on a taco Tuesday night, in sipping coffee with a friend, in watching our parents age, in sitting in business meetings or on the front porch swing. Every experience in which we can glorify God is a place that God is still shaping and molding us into the image of His Son. This is how the Holy Spirit grows the fruit of the Spirit in us. By abiding in Him, by continually becoming, we learn to hear and discern God's voice and His will for us. As we keep a simple and pure devotion to Christ, the fruit of the Spirit begins to blossom.

> **We don't have to try to force the simple life; we accept it as a sacred rhythm for our daily lives.**

List the fruit of the Spirit from Galatians 5:22–23.

In what ways does living a simple life produce and grow the fruit of the Spirit?

Think about your life when you started this study six weeks ago and look at it now. In what ways can you see the Holy Spirit working in your life, ripening the fruit that makes us like Jesus?

Paul helps explain this idea of transformation in 2 Corinthians:

> Since, then, we have such a hope, we act with great boldness. . . . Now the LORD is the Spirit, and where the Spirit of the LORD is, there is freedom. We all, with unveiled faces, are looking as in a mirror at the glory of the LORD and *are being transformed* into the same image from glory to glory; this is from the LORD who is the Spirit. (3:12, 17–18)

As you consider 2 Corinthians 3:17–18, what explanation do you see for your continual transformation?

From the beginning of our study, we've looked at abiding in Christ as a courageous way for us to embrace a lifestyle of simplicity. Hopefully, we have experienced glimpses of simplicity and feelings of greater peace and rest as we've made our way together through these weeks. But we can't expect to "arrive" at being a woman of simplicity. That can make us feel impatient—*Why am I not experiencing the simple life I thought I was going to have by now?* Living in the peace of the present, understanding that we are still becoming, still transforming, means that we wait with hope for what is to come. Isaiah 30:18 tells us,

> The LORD is waiting to show you mercy,
> and is rising up to show you compassion,
> for the LORD is a just God.
> All who wait patiently for him are happy.

In this sense, happiness comes out of the simplicity of waiting on the Lord.

Throughout the Bible, we read of God telling us to wait on Him. What does He promise for us when we do?

    Psalm 27:13–14

    Psalm 33:20–22

    Psalm 40:1–17

    Isaiah 40:31

As Kaitlyn so rightly expressed at the beginning of today's study, we're part of the greatest story ever told. It's a simple story—one that doesn't get muddied up with the distractions we mistakenly believe we must do or be. It's the story of God transforming us into Christlikeness as we are still and simply know that He is God. So we can metaphorically (or literally) light our candles to remind us that the Light of the world is at work in our lives, pushing back the darkness and displaying the beauty of the ordinary and mundane.

Do you struggle with waiting? Explain.

In what ways do you think waiting on the Lord transforms you into a woman of simplicity?

Reread Philippians 3:12. How does the message there offer you freedom? Simplicity? Peace?

What does this verse mean for how you might courageously live differently today?

Reflect on this prayer and make it your own today:

Lord, thank You that You are still working in me, still transforming me into a woman of simplicity, into a woman who reflects and glorifies Jesus. Help me to wait patiently through the process. Grow my trust and dependence, knowing that You are growing the beautiful fruit of Your Spirit within me. Amen.

He renews my life;
he leads me along the right paths
for his name's sake.

Psalm 23:3

I've been claustrophobic since preschool. That's probably where my fear of being stuck in small spaces began. My only memory from that early year of school is being chased by a little boy with sandy-colored curls on top of his head. His goal was to pull my long black hair as hard as he could.

My hair was like a matador's muleta waving across the playground, provoking this preschooler who seemed more bull than boy. I ran from him every recess and hid in a tiny playhouse where I squished my body against the back wall.

When my husband and I bought our first home, he made a comment about needing to stay put for at least ten years. When I heard "ten years," the claustrophobia crept down into my soul. I felt my spirit fold like a piece of origami that's been pressed until its seams are permanent. I didn't want to commit to this simple Midwestern suburban neighborhood. Committing made me feel like I was losing control. What if we missed out on what we wanted by staying here? I wanted our family to be able to grow and unfold and stretch its wings wide.

Well-meaning acquaintances said our new home reminded them of their starter home a few homes back. I heard others talk about the kind of spaces that worked best for hospitality, and our home didn't fit the description. I wondered if we could find community in a place where conversations rarely escaped topics like yardwork and how busy the main street was becoming. Scarcity became the matador waving its red muleta in front of my heart, making me question if there would be enough here to be all that I thought we should have in a place.

More than ten years later, we still live in our first (and only) home, on the same unremarkable cul-de-sac that blends right into our neighborhood along with every other neighborhood in the area. It's an easily forgettable street from the outside, but it's full of people we've come to love deeply and who've loved us in return.

I've since learned that matadors only wave the red muleta in the final stages of a bullfight, when victory is in their grasp. I've also learned that there's no place too small, plain, or forgettable, where love won't reach. The simplicity that I feared would keep me stuck forever has only helped to set me free.

—TASHA JUN

Have you ever felt stuck in a place, home, or mental state? What helped set you free?

_____

_____

_____

_____

There's a lot to simplicity, isn't there? Or at least it probably feels that way! And yet if we boil it all down, it really is "simply" about giving ourselves fully to God. It's believing what Psalm 23:3 tells us: "[My Shepherd] renews my life; he leads me along the right paths for his name's sake." The Lord directs our paths through all kinds of terrain—busy places, turmoil, the valley of the shadow of death—but this truth remains steadfast: He provides, He protects, He directs. All we have to do is follow. As Psalm 119:73 says, "You made me; you created me. Now give me the sense to follow your commands" (NLT).

If you want a life of rest, follow the Good Shepherd.

If you want a life of joy, follow the Good Shepherd.

If you want a life of peace, follow the Good Shepherd.

If you want a life that isn't complicated and pressured, follow the Good Shepherd.

Abandon everything else—everything the world tells you to be, to have, to do—and follow the Good Shepherd. He will renew your life and will guide you for a bigger purpose than you can possibly imagine. He wants you to courageously pursue a single-minded devotion to Him.

Will God's plans always be what we would choose? No. But does anyone know what's best for us more than the God who created us and loves us?

This is simplicity at its finest: courageously abandoning ourselves, boldly choosing to let the Holy Spirit live in us and have His way with us, walking in the way of Jesus, obeying the God we love, and embracing that we are enough based on who we are in Christ. To get to the end of our lives and be able to say, along with David, "My steps have stayed on your path; I have not wavered from following you" (Ps. 17:5 NLT) . . . there is no better way.

Think about your old self, your life before following Jesus. What did you give up in order to become a new creation in Christ?

With that understanding, does it make it easier or harder to give up control of your life, to abandon yourself and follow Jesus?

Our Good Shepherd leads us into a simpler life for our good *and* for His glory. Think about all the benefits of simplicity we've unpacked over the last six weeks. Living out simplicity brings us health and contentment, it brings a depth to our relationships, it allows us to better hear our Shepherd's voice. But simplicity isn't just transforming us internally—it's shining a spotlight on the kind of life only God can give. How different our lives look to the rest of the world when we live a simpler life for His name's sake. As the world runs at nonstop, supersonic speed levels—becoming more and more desperate for peace, grasping at the emptiness and superficial things that never satisfy and lead only to more striving—we live a different way. We have the opportunity to display the Savior's answer to a broken and fallen world.

We have the opportunity to display the Savior's answer to a broken and fallen world.

Jesus offers a simpler life for a greater purpose than just our own happiness. We reap contentment and peace when we embrace simplicity—and then our lives show others what Jesus can do for them as well. We don't do this by taking on more ministry or serving until we drop from exhaustion. We do this by living simply.

How do the following verses encourage you to keep pursuing a life with God at the very center?

Psalm 27:8

Romans 12:1

Galatians 2:19–20

_____

_____

_____

_____

The Lord wants to lead you. He wants your undivided attention. He wants you to know that "we are God's masterpiece. He has created us anew in Christ Jesus, so we can do the good things he planned for us long ago" (Eph. 2:10 NLT). He wants you to give yourself completely to Him, listen to His voice, follow wherever He takes you. This is how you become a courageous woman of simplicity, a woman who can confidently testify, "The LORD is my shepherd; I have what I need" (Ps. 23:1).

Reflect on all you have learned throughout these past six weeks. What has stood out most to you about simplicity? What has surprised you?

_____

_____

_____

_____

Reflect on this prayer and make it your own today:

Lord, may I ever hear Your voice and follow without argument. May I pursue simplicity with abandon. Above all, may I glorify You through leading a life of simple and pure devotion to my Savior, Jesus Christ. Amen.

notes

Week 1 A Plea for Simplicity

1. Donald S. Whitney, *Simplify Your Spiritual Life* (Colorado Springs, CO: NavPress, 2003), 26.
2. Michele W. Berger, "Social Media Use Increases Depression and Loneliness," PennToday, November 9, 2018, https://penntoday.upenn.edu/news/social-media-use-increases-depression-and-loneliness.

Week 2 What Drives Us

1. "Mexican Fisherman Story" is a commonly adapted parable from Heinrich Böll, "Anecdote Concerning the Lowering of Productivity," *The Stories of Heinrich Böll* (Evanston, IL: Northwestern University Press, 1995), 628–30. Originally published in 1963.
2. Richard J. Foster, *Celebration of Discipline: The Path to Spiritual Growth*, 25th anniversary ed. (San Francisco: HarperSanFrancisco, 1998), 83.

Week 3 Living in the Sacred Present

1. Matthew Henry, "Psalm 46," *Matthew Henry's Commentary*, Biblegateway.com, accessed January 28, 2020, https://www.biblegateway.com/resources/matthew-henry/Ps.46.1-Ps.46.11.
2. "Psalm 46," *Reformation Study Bible*, Biblegateway.com, accessed January 28, 2020, https://www.biblegateway.com/resources/reformation-study-bible/Ps.46.
3. Stuart Briscoe, "When Trouble Comes—Psalm 46," Preaching.com, accessed January 28, 2020, https://www.preaching.com/sermons/when-trouble-comes-psalm-46/.

Week 4 Being Enough

1. *Encyclopedia Britannica Online*, s.v. "Gamaliel I," accessed April 16, 2020, https://www.britannica.com/biography/Gamaliel-I.
2. Annie S. Hawks, "I Need Thee Every Hour," 1872.
3. Nelson Glueck, *Hesed in the Bible* (1967; repr. Eugene, OR: Wipf & Stock, 2011), 8.

Week 5 Open-Hands Living

1. *Holman Bible Dictionary*, s.v. "Obedience," accessed February 4, 2020, https://www.studylight.org/dictionaries/hbd/o/obedience.html.

2. Thomas D. Thurman, "Jesus Teaches His Way," *Standard Lesson Commentary, 1976–77* (Cincinnati: Standard Publishing, 1976), 257.

3. Marie Kondo, *Spark Joy: An Illustrated Master Class on the Art of Organizing and Tidying Up* (New York: New Speed Press, 2016).

4. "Marie Kondo on How to Recognize What Sparks Joy," *Parade*, December 23, 2015, https://parade.com/445589/parade/marie-kondo-on-how-to-recognize-what-sparks-joy/.

5. KonMari: The Official Website of Marie Kondo, https://konmari.com/.

Week 6 Embracing the Peace That Comes

1. C. H. Spurgeon, *The Treasury of David* (Toronto: Funk & Wagnalls, 1882), 63.

2. Matthew Henry, "1 Chronicles 4," *Matthew Henry Commentary on the Whole Bible*, accessed February 8, 2020, https://www.biblestudytools.com/commentaries/matthew-henry-complete/1-chronicles/4.html.

3. John Piper, "How Do I Pray the Bible?," Desiring God, February 6, 2017, https://www.desiringgod.org/interviews/how-do-i-pray-the-bible.

about the authors

Ginger Kolbaba is a bestselling, award-winning author, editor, and speaker. She has written or contributed to more than thirty-five books, including *Breakthrough*, recently released as a major motion picture. She is a sassy contemplative and a fun-loving traveler who loves Jesus most of all. Visit her at gingerkolbaba.com.

Karina Allen is devoted to helping women live out their unique calling and building authentic community through practical application of Scripture in an approachable, winsome manner. Connect with her on Instagram @karina268.

Lucretia Berry is the creator of Brownicity.com. She is a wife, mom of three, and a former college professor whose passion for racial healing led her to author *What LIES between Us: Fostering First Steps toward Racial Healing* and to speak at TEDx Charlotte and Q Ideas Charlotte. Find her at brownicity.com and on Instagram @lucretiaberry.

Kaitlyn Bouchillon is a writer who is learning to see God's goodness in the beautiful ordinary of right now. She is the author of *Even If Not: Living, Loving, and Learning in the in Between*, and she'll never turn down an iced latte. Find her at kaitlynbouchillon.com and on Instagram @kaitlyn_bouch.

Stephanie Bryant is the cofounder of (in)courage and hosts the *Jesus Led Adventure* podcast. She enjoys spending her days with her husband and their miracle daughter on their farm. Find Stephanie on Instagram @StephanieSBryant and at stephaniebryant.me.

Grace P. Cho is the (in)courage editorial manager. In the middle of her years in church ministry, she sensed God moving her toward writing, to use her words to lead. She coaches writers, mentors leaders, and believes that telling our stories can change the world. Connect with her on Instagram @gracepcho.

Holley Gerth is a bestselling author who loves encouraging the hearts of women through words. She does so through her books like *You're Already Amazing* and *Fiercehearted*. Holley is a beloved daughter of God, wife to Mark, Mama to Lovelle, and Nana to Ellie and Clem. Find her at holleygerth.com and on Instagram @holleygerth.

Bonnie Gray is the author of *Whispers of Rest* and *Finding Spiritual Whitespace*, a wife, and mom to two boys. An inspirational speaker featured at Relevant Magazine and Christianity Today, she's guided thousands to detox stress and experience God's love through soul care. Find her at TheBonnieGray.com and on Instagram @thebonniegray.

Tasha Jun is a dreamer, a Hapa girl, wife to Matt, and mama to three little tender warriors. A coffee drinker, storyteller, and kimchi eater, she was made to walk where cultures collide, on dirt roads and carefully placed cobblestone streets. Jesus is her heartbeat. Find her on Instagram @tashajunb and at tashajun.com.

Becky Keife is the (in)courage community manager. As a speaker, she shares vulnerably real stories and biblical wisdom, and she's the author of *No Better Mom for the Job*. Becky loves hiking sunny trails with her husband and three spirited sons. Connect with her on Instagram @beckykeife and at beckykeife.com.

Aliza Latta is a Canadian writer, journalist, and artist, who is a huge fan of telling stories. She writes about faith and young adulthood at alizalatta.com, and is the author of the novel *Come Find Me, Sage Parker*. Find her on Instagram @alizalatta.

Patricia Raybon, an award-winning author and journalist, grew up in a time of hate but found God's love in a time of need. Serving from Colorado, she writes on faith, race, and grace—seeking to inspire healing in Christ. Join her on the journey at patriciaraybon.com.

Anna Rendell is the (in)courage digital content manager and lives in Minnesota with her husband and their kids. She loves a good book and a great latte. Anna is the author of *Pumpkin Spice for Your Soul* and *A Moment of Christmas*. Visit her at AnnaRendell.com and on Instagram @annaerendell.

Michelle Reyes, PhD, is an Indian American pastor's wife, writer, and activist. She is vice president of the Asian American Christian Collaborative and writes regularly on faith, culture, and justice. Michelle lives in Austin, TX, with her husband and two kids. Follow her on Instagram @michelleamireyes.

Experience True Joy Right Where You Are

If you want to be able to "rejoice in the Lord always" not just in theory but in everyday practice, if you long for a profound sense of calm and confidence in every season and situation of life, this 6-week study will light the way.

100 Days of Hope and Peace

In this 100-day devotional, the (in)courage community comes alongside you when your heart is grieving, your faith is shaking, or it's just one of those mundane hard days. Each day includes a key Scripture, a heartening devotion, and a prayer to remind you that God is near and hope is possible.

(in)courage welcomes you

to a place where authentic, brave women
connect deeply with God and others.
Through the power of shared stories and
meaningful resources, (in)courage champions
women and celebrates the strength Jesus gives
to live out our calling as God's daughters.
In the middle of your unfine moments
and ordinary days, you are invited to
become a woman of courage.

Join us at **www.incourage.me**
& connect with us on social media!